The Kabuki Guide

The

KODANSHA INTERNATIONAL
Tokyo and New York

Kabuki Guide

Text by **Masakatsu Gunji**

Photography by **Chiaki Yoshida**

Translation by **Christopher Holmes**

Note: Japanese names, other than those on the title page, are given in the traditional Japanese order, surname preceding given name.

Cover illustrations: The front cover shows the courtesan Agemaki (as played by Bandō Tamasaburō) in the play *Sukeroku Yukari no Edo Zakura*; the back, the chivalrous commoner Sukeroku (Ichikawa Danjūrō) in the same play.

Half-title page: The Entrance to a Kabuki theater. *Shibai Kimmō Zui* (Illustrated Encyclopedia of Kabuki), first published in 1803.

Title pages: Billboards in front of the Ichimura-za, in Edo, at the time of the "face-showing" performance in November, which traditionally marked the beginning of a new theatrical season. *Shibai Kimmō Zui* (Illustrated Encyclopedia of Kabuki, first published in 1803.

Pages 6–7. Crowds bustle in front of the teahouses that surrounded Kabuki theaters: in this case during a "face-showing" performance, which were customarily held in November and signified the start of a new Kabuki season.

Distributed in the United States by Kodansha International/USA Ltd., through Harper and Row Publishers, Inc., 10 East 53rd Street, New York, New York 10022. Published by Kodansha International Ltd., 2-2 Otowa 1-chome, Bunkyo-ku, Tokyo 112 and Kodansha International/USA Ltd., 10 East 53rd Street, New York, New York 10022.

LCC 87-81678
ISBN 0-87011-847-1 (USA)
ISBN 4-7700-1347-7 (Japan)
First edition, 1987

CONTENTS

Thirty-six Plays: Synopses and Highlights 58

1. Screen painting of Kabuki as performed by women in the
Keichō era (1596–1615). Detail.

2. *Shibaraku* (Wait!). Hidden assistants hold out the sleeves of Kamakura no Gongorō as he poses on the main stage.

4. *Sukeroku Yukari no Edo Zakura* (Sukeroku, Flower of Edo). Sukeroku, having concluded his dance of entry on the *hanamichi*, proceeds to the main stage, where he strikes a final pose with his umbrella.

3. *Narukami* (Narukami the Priest). Enraged at his seduction by Princess Taema, Narukami is transformed into the God of Thunder. He stands poised at the foot of the *hanamichi* ready to give chase.

5

6

5. *Sugawara Denju Tenarai Kagami* (Sugawara's Secrets of Calligraphy), act 4, scene 3, "The Village School." To deceive the enemy, Matsuō-maru declares that the severed head of his own son is that of Sugawara's child, whom is is trying to protect.

6. *Ichinotani Futaba Gunki* (Chronicle of the Battle of Ichinotani), act 2, scene 3, "Another Part of the Beach." Kumagai agonizes as he prepares to behead what appears to be an enemy prince but is, in fact, his own son, whom he has been forced to substitute at the last minute.

7. *Kanadehon Chūshingura* (The Treasury of Loyal Retainers), act 9, "The House of Yuranosuke at Yamashina." Konami prepares to die at the hand of her mother, Tonase, who then intends to commit suicide. Konami's father, Honzō, lingers in the background disguised as a mendicant priest.

8. *Aoto Zōshi Hana no Nishiki-e* (The Gang of Five), act 3, "The Hamamatsuya Kimono Store." Benten Kozō throws off his woman's disguise and reveals his true identity. At the same time, he displays his left arm and shoulder, covered in a vivid tattoo.

9. *Tōkaidō Yotsuya Kaidan* (Yotsuya Ghost Stories), act 2, "The House of Tamiya Iemon." Iemon looks in horror at the face of his wife, Oiwa.

10. *Kosode Soga Azami no Ironui* (The Tale of Izayoi and Seishin), act 1, scene 1, "The Hyapponkui Dike by Inase River." The two lovers, one a courtesan and the other a priest, share a final, ritualistic drink of water before committing suicide together.

11. *Musume Dōjōji* (The Maiden at Dōjōji Temple). Having transformed itself into a dancing girl, the vengeful spirit of Kiyohime looks up at the temple bell it has come to destroy.

12. *Kasane* (Disfigured Kasane). Kasane expresses her love for Yoemon, not realizing that he is the murderer of her father.

THE
DEVELOPMENT
OF
KABUKI

The word *kabuki*, as it is used today, refers exclusively to the Japanese theatrical art of the name, which now exists as a combination of music, dance, and drama performed against stage settings that are frequently spectacular. At the turn of sixteenth century, however, when Kabuki had its beginnings, the word was in use as part and parcel of everyday speech and with quite a different meaning.

Deriving from the verb *kabuku*—"to incline," "to tilt," "to lean to one side"—*kabuki* signified "unusual" and "unconventional," in relation particularly to certain social trends of the time that were disapproved of as excessively unorthodox. These trends also involved certain extravagances in dress and behavior, so that *kabuki* also connoted "fashionable" and "faddish," even "avant-garde."

Kabuki theater came into existence at the beginning of the historical epoch known as the Edo, or Tokugawa, period (1603–1867). Following in the wake of catastrophic civil wars that wracked the country for more than a century, this period has been called the Pax Tokugawa, characterized as it was by continued peace and stability under the Tokugawa shogunate. But its early years were also a time of great confusion, as a result of which townspeople turned to the eccentric or unconventional for distraction. This phenomenon is reflected in the word *kabuki* itself, which was a product of this 17 state of affairs. *Kabuki* then became an abbreviation of "*kabuki* dance," a type of entertainment which, by exceeding conventional norms, was thought of as new, unusual, and exciting. From such primitive origins as these, Kabuki developed to become the most important and dynamic theatrical art of the Edo period.

Kabuki differs in two important respects from the classical performing arts that preceded it. The first is that, while the predecessors of Kabuki consisted of either masked drama or masked dance-drama, in Kabuki the mask does not figure at all. Significantly, this rejection of the mask was not merely a technical innovation. It represented the birth of interest in the human form, the discovery of the beauty and fascination of the human body. What is more, this important discovery was made by women—not men—despite their inferior, unprivileged position in society. By discarding the mask, the women who were the founders of Kabuki prefigured the dawning of a modern sensibility toward the human figure, just as the dawn of the Edo period marks the beginning of modern Japanese history.

Dance is the second major difference between Kabuki and its predecessors. At the heart of the classical performing arts was the stately dance form known as *mai*, characterized by slow, horizontal circling movements, the soles of the feet hardly leaving the surface of the stage. Early Kabuki, however, went to the opposite extreme by following the lively folk-dance tradition, *odori*, involving more energetic vertical movements and even jumps. Previously regarded as unartistic, it was through Kabuki that *odori* was transformed into art.

According to historical records, Kabuki began in 1603 with the dances performed by the woman who is regarded as the founder of Kabuki, Izumo no Okuni, at Shijōgawara, in the city of Kyoto. One account describes Okuni as performing a folk dance while striking a small gong. Attracted by the sound, the ghost of a certain Nagoya Sanza, who, before his death in a quarrel, had been notorious for his outrageously *kabuki* behavior, would appear on the stage and the two would dance hand in hand. The popularity of teahouses and bath-houses (both a type of bordello) at that time is reflected in the Kabuki dances of Okuni in which she would appear in the guise of a male customer, fantastically attired, at such establishments. That she would also have a crucifix dangling from her waist or neck as an accessory was all part of the strangeness and appeal of early Kabuki.

As Okuni's Kabuki dances became more popular, they attracted imitators, who formed troupes of their own and began to tour the country. These troupes were composed of women who were prostitutes as much as anything else, and for this reason the Kabuki of this period is now referred to as Prostitutes' (*yūjo*) Kabuki or, more innocuously, Women's (*onna*) Kabuki (fig. 1). The Tokugawa shogunate, however, disapproved, and in 1629 such troupes were banned. At the same time, a law went into force forbidding women to appear on the stage, which had a profound influence on the subsequent development of Kabuki.

Women's Kabuki was succeeded by Boys' (*wakashu*) Kabuki, comprising troupes of attractive youths, but in 1652 this too was banned on the grounds of immorality.

Boys' Kabuki was succeeded by Men's (*yarō*) Kabuki. But in order to distinguish it from its notorious predecessors, it could only be performed under the name "Plays Imitating Manners and Customs" (*monomane kyōgen zukushi*). In this form Men's Kabuki flourished to become the historical precursor of Kabuki as it exists today.

KABUKI
THEATERS

The Playhouse

The number of officially sanctioned Kabuki theaters in the
Edo period was limited to four each in Osaka, Kyoto, and
Edo (present-day Tokyo). In Edo, however, the number was
later reduced to three. The special status of these theaters was
indicated by a small tower (*yagura*) erected on the roof (fig.
13). These towers no longer exist, but temporary ones are
erected over the main entrances of the Kabuki-za in Tokyo
(fig. 14) and the Minami-za in Kyoto, for the special performances given at those theaters in November and December,
respectively. Only those theaters with an official tower had
the right to be managed on a hereditary basis, a prerogative
called "tower authority." The tower, which is still part of
Sumo wrestling today, contained a Shinto shrine and a drum
that signaled the start of the day's performances. Like Sumo
arenas at that time, the central seating area in early theaters
was roofless—only the stage and box seats were sheltered from
rain. As a result, performances would be canceled in incle-
ment weather. It was not until the Kyōhō era (1716–36)
that all Kabuki theaters were completely covered. As for the
Kabuki stage itself, it was modeled on that of the Noh theater,
only gradually developing into the form it takes today.

20

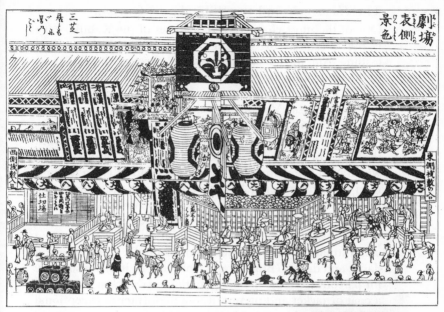

13. Facade of a Kabuki Theater showing official tower (top, center). From *Shibai Kimmō Zui* (Illustrated Encyclopedia of Kabuki), first published in 1803.

14. A temporary official tower of the Kabuki-za in Tokyo, in place for the annual gala production in November.

The *Hanamichi* and the "Standard" Curtain

One of the most characteristic features of the Kabuki stage is the *hanamichi*, or "flower path"—a raised passageway leading from the left side of the stage, through the audience, to the back of the theater. It serves as a means of entry, and exit, to and from the main stage, and also as a secondary stage in its own right. Various theories have been proposed concerning the origins of the *hanamichi*. The most influential traces it to the Noh stage, that is, to the passageway leading from the "mirror" (i.e., green) room to the stage proper along which Noh actors make their entrances and exits. In the opinion of some experts, however, including the author, the rudimentary form of the *hanamichi* is to be found in the small flight of steps at the front of the Noh stage (fig. 15).

The *hana* ("flower") of *hanamichi* referred originally to a congratulatory gift or present. For example, when enjoying dance and drama (Bugaku and Noh, that is) it was customary for patrons from the nobility and the warrior class to remove a coat or jacket and present it to a performer of exceptional skill. Draping the gift around his shoulders, the recipient would then perform another dance in celebration. In time, performers were given actual flowers (sprays of plum blossom) to which were attached a list of the presents they would later receive. Eventually, the word "flower" acquired the further meaning of "a gift of money." It is likely, therefore, that the original "flower path" was the pathway along which spectators made their way, from their seats to the stage, to present actors with real or monetary "flowers." It was not until 1716 that the *hanamichi* came into use as an acting area.

One of the principal functions of the *hanamichi* is to highlight entrances and exits. For this reason, when actors arrive or leave, they will stop at a point known as the "seven-three" (*shichi-san*)—so called because its location is seven tenths the length of the *hanamichi* from the back of the theater and three tenths from the main stage—to pose, speak, or dance. While 22 it is commonly said that the extent of an actor's ability is ob-

15. A Noh stage. According to some experts, the Kabuki *hanamichi* derives from the flight of steps at the front.

vious from the moment he steps on the stage, the *hanamichi* provides a special opportunity for actors to demonstrate their talents to the audience, those of dance and movement particularly. It is in this idea that the rationale of the *hanamichi* lies, and two of the best examples are those of Benkei's powerful exit at the end of *Kanjinchō* (The Subscription Scroll; fig. 16), and the dance that Sukeroku performs when he first makes his entry in the play of that name (fig. 17).

On the one hand, therefore, the *hanamichi* is a pathway to and from the stage, often representing a road or river in the course of a play. On the other, its function is that of a separate acting area or secondary stage. In *Kanjinchō*, for instance, the *hanamichi* comes into its own as a stage *after* the curtain has been drawn on the main stage and the action there is over. Moreover, another (temporary) *hanamichi* is sometimes erected on the right side of the auditorium, parallel to the permanent one, to serve as an additional pathway or stage (fig. 18).

Another feature characteristic of Kabuki is its use of curtains. In Japanese classical drama and dance, curtains were relatively little used, and in Kabuki they came into existence 23

16. *Kanjinchō*. Benkei prepares to make his "six-directions" exit along the *hanamichi* at the conclusion of the play.

17. *Sukeroku Yukari no Edo Za-kura*. Sukeroku, the chivalrous commoner, during his dance of entry.

only around 1664. Before that, performances of Kabuki had consisted of programs of individual dances and dramatic sketches with comic pantomimes in between. With the advent of the curtain, however, longer plays were created in which a single plot tied together a number of consecutive scenes or acts. It was from this point that Kabuki began to progress as a theatrical art.

The main Kabuki curtain, drawn from the side rather than lowered from above, was conventionally patterned in broad

18. *Imoseyama Onna Teikin*, act 3, scene 3, "The Mountains." A temporary *hanamichi* (at bottom) has been erected for the entrances of Daihanji and Sadaka, who walk along the banks of the river that is indicated on the stage.

vertical stripes of persimmon, green, and black, as it is today (fig. 3). This custom was followed especially in the theaters of Edo. Called *jōshikimaku*, or "standard curtain," its use was restricted during the Edo period to licensed establishments with a tower. Such curtains were objects of enormous pride, both as symbols of authority and as marks of prestige. In contrast, unlicensed establishments had to be satisfied with a drop curtain called a *donchō*. As a result, performances at those establishments were contemptuously referred to as *donchō* drama.

The Kabuki curtain is also unusual for the way it is opened and closed and the timing this involves. In this connection, it is worth mentioning a performance of *Kanjinchō* in the United States some years ago. When the main curtain was closed, the audience assumed the play to be over and prepared to leave, not realizing that the climax was yet to come. In Kabuki, the fact that the curtain has been drawn does not necessarily mean the end of a scene, act, or play. In this respect, the Kabuki curtain is quite different from curtains in other theatrical traditions. Thus, in *Kanjinchō*, it is *after* the 25 main curtain has been drawn that the hero, Benkei, makes his spectacular exit along the *hanamichi* (fig. 16) and disappears behind the small *agemaku* curtain at the back of the auditorium. Not until then, when the *agemaku* curtain has closed after Benkei, does the play come to an end.

Incidentally, the *agemaku* (literally, "raised curtain") is not raised, as the name suggests, but opened and closed from the side. Despite this, it is not referred to as a "draw curtain" (*hikimaku*) because it would then be confused with the draw curtain on the main stage. Another reason is that the name *agemaku* derives historically from a similar curtain used in Noh drama.

Another Kabuki curtain, employed for dramatic effect, is the *asagimaku* ("pale-blue" curtain). In this case, the curtain, already suspended over the stage, is released from above when two wooden clappers are struck, so that it drops suddenly to the floor to reveal a new and impressive scene behind. In other words, the effect is similar to that of a sudden "cut" in a motion picture. Here, again, a Kabuki curtain is employed in a way not seen anywhere else, and a good example is that of the Suma Beach scene in the play *Ichinotani Futaba Gunki* (Chronicle of the Battle of Ichinotani). The use of the *asagimaku* is particularly successful here, not only for the visual effect of the sudden revelation of the seashore and the ocean beyond, but also as a means of suggesting to the audience that a powerful piece of drama is to follow—the decapitation by Kumagai of his own beloved son.

Actors' Positioning on the Stage

A further characteristic of Kabuki concerns certain conventions regarding the positioning of actors on the stage. The right-hand side of the stage (as seen from the audience) is called, in Japanese, *kami-te* (literally, "upper hand") and the left-hand side, *shimo-te* ("lower hand"). Although actors may occasionally enter from the right, this is unusual. The convention is that entrances are made from the left, by way of

26

the *hanamichi*. The rationale for this is that the right-hand side of the stage, *kami-te*, is related to *kami-za* ("upper seat"), the place of honor reserved for guests or personages of high rank. Thus the right-hand side of the stage, like the seat of honor, is an exalted area to be treated with respect.

This explains why imperial messengers and other official envoys, having entered from the left, invariably cross to the right of the stage and take up their positions there. Similarly, when both men and women are seated on the stage, the men are always positioned on the right.

Terakoya (The Village School) provides a good example of how psychological tension can be created by nothing more than the actors changing places on the stage. In this particular play, the envoy Matsuōmaru enters from the left and crosses to the right side of the stage, which is already occupied by his enemy, Genzō, the principal of the school. At the same time Genzō, who has no choice but to give way, begins to move warily to the left. The suspense of this moment, as each man tries to fathom the intentions of the other, is impressive.

Another convention requires that actors of female roles neither walk nor sit in front of male-role actors during a performance, but always take a position behind. Similarly, should a group of characters in a play be seated in a line across the stage, the women will always sit on the left, an Edo-period custom adopted into Kabuki and still adhered to.

The Revolving Stage and the Trap Lift

The revolving stage, which can now be seen in Western theaters and boasts an especially long history in Germany, is a Kabuki invention attributed to the playwright Namiki Shōzō (1730–73) and derived, it is said, from the principle of a spinning top. Originally a circular wooden platform placed and rotated on the main stage, the revolving stage was first used in 1758 in a vendetta play by Namiki that is, however, no longer performed. The play concluded with an act of revenge being simultaneously carried out in two dif- 27 ferent locations, and the desire to show this on the stage led to the idea of constructing two sets, one on each half of a circular wooden base that could be rotated at will (fig. 19).

Later, a bull's-eye (*janome*) revolving stage was also developed. Consisting of two circles, one inside the other, that could be moved in opposite directions at the same time, it enjoyed a certain popularity but is now no longer used in Kabuki.

The revolving stage as it exists today is set into the main stage itself and is level with it. The machinery for the revolving stage is accommodated deep beneath the main stage in an area known as *naraku* ("hell"). Trap lifts of various sizes are incorporated into the revolving stage, allowing for sudden appearances and disappearances of both actors and scenery. There is also a small trap lift in the *hanamichi*, just before it reaches the main stage, and this is mainly used for the entrances of ghosts, magicians, and other supernatural beings (fig. 20).

19. A change of scene taking place by means of the revolving stage. From *Shibai Kimmō Zui* (Illustrated Encyclopedia of Kabuki), first published in 1803.

20. An actor coming into view on the *hanamichi* by means of a trap lift. From *Shibai Kimmō Zui* (Illustrated Encyclopedia of Kabuki), first published in 1803.

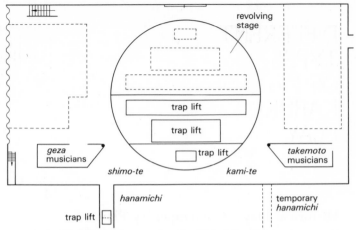

21. Plan of a present-day Kabuki stage.

The Stage upon the Stage

A second stage—a kind of stage upon the stage—is a feature of dances and dance-dramas in Kabuki. Made of cypress wood, it consists of raised rectangular sections that are laid over the main stage, and often along the whole length of the *hanamichi* as well. The purpose of this temporary stage is not only to facilitate movement, but also to enhance the sound of the foot stamping that is fundamental to Kabuki dance.

During the course of a Kabuki play, the background music issues from a small room at the left-hand side of the stage. In dances, however, the musicians involved appear in full view of the audience, their position on the stage depending upon the type of accompaniment they provide. In the singing style known as *nagauta* ("long song"), the musicians—consisting of singers, shamisen players, drummers, and a flutist—sit facing the audience on a tiered platform, covered in red felt, at the back of the stage. If the accompaniment is of the narrative, *jōruri*, type, the musicians (chanters and shamisen players only) sit at one side of the stage on a dais set at an angle to the audience. Whether the dais is positioned at the right or left side of the stage depends on the type of *jōruri* involved.   29

DIFFERENT TYPES OF KABUKI PLAY

Historical Plays, Contemporary Plays

Generally speaking, Kabuki plays can be divided into two main categories: *jidaimono* (''period'' or ''historical'' plays) and *sewamono* (''contemporary'' plays). Historical plays are those set in any epoch earlier than that of the Edo period (1603–1867) and which portray the lives of warriors and aristocrats. Contemporary plays are set in the Edo period itself. Frequently based on actual events—a sensational murder, a case of adultery, the suicide of a pair of lovers—the protagonists are always ordinary people.

An important point to remember in connection with historical plays is that it was forbidden by the authorities to dramatize for the Kabuki stage current events involving the shogunate itself or the military and upper classes. This stricture was easily circumvented, however, by transposing such events, slightly disguised, to an earlier historical period. Thus *Kanadehon Chūshingura* (The Treasury of Loyal Retainers), for example, first staged in 1748, takes as it subject an actual vendetta from the Edo period, but represents it as having occurred in the Ashikaga period (1336–1573). This simple expedient fooled no one but was apparently sufficient to satisfy the censors.

Geographical locations could undergo a similar transposition, so that a scene set ostensibly in Kamakura would be

22. A Kabuki rehearsal in progress. From *Shibai Kimmō Zui* (Illustrated Encyclopedia of Kabuki), first published in 1803.

understood to be actually taking place in Edo. The purpose of this, once again, was to avoid official interference, and a typical example is found in the play *Aoto Zōshi Hana no Nishiki-e* (The Gang of Five). According to the script, the famous "Mustering" scene (fig. 35)—in which the thieves, dressed in brilliantly colored kimonos, make elaborate speeches in defiance of the troop of police officers who come to arrest them—takes place by the river Inase in Kamakura. Yet the actual setting—as one glance of the stage tells the audience—is obviously that of the river Sumida in Edo.

An important point to remember in connection with traditional plays—especially those of the historical type—is that many were originally written for Bunraku, the theater of puppets that developed together with Kabuki and influenced it greatly. This explains the presence, in Bunraku-derived Kabuki plays, of a chanter or narrator who sits on a dais at the right of the stage accompanied by a player of the shamisen. In Bunraku, the narrator speaks all the lines for the puppets and everything else besides. In Kabuki, the actors speak their own lines, so the role of the narrator is much diminished but nonetheless an essential one. And the shamisen provides the 31 play's fundamental rhythms to which the actors time their movements and speeches.

The combination of narrator and shamisen player is called *chobo* or *takemoto* (after Takemoto Gidayū, who created this style of accompaniment in the seventeenth century). If a play has no *takemoto* accompaniment, it is reasonably safe to assume that it is "pure" Kabuki and not an adaptation from Bunraku. But this rule does not apply to later works written in the nineteenth century, when Kabuki playwrights were sometimes fond of incorporating *takemoto*, for its own sake, into their plays.

The distinction between historical and contemporary play is also important in the arrangement of a day's program of Kabuki. In the past it was the rule that the first item of the day be a historical and the second a contemporary play. Today, it is not necessary to adhere so strictly to this convention, but in practice most theaters still do. The reason for this doubtless derives from the contrast between formality and informality that is to be found in many of the traditional Japanese performing arts. Thus the first, historical play is characterized by ceremonial and stylization. The second, contemporary play is remarkable for its relaxed atmosphere and absence of ceremony. A similar state of affairs exists in classical Noh theater, in which a serious and stately dance-drama is followed by an amusing Kyōgen farce. The juxtaposition of the formal and the informal, it would seem, is fundamental to classical Japanese performing arts.

Despite the nature of contemporary (*sewamono*) plays and their position on the program, they are in fact an older category than that of the historical (*jidaimono*) play, since the word *sewamono* came into existence first and there is documentary evidence to prove it. It was only toward the end of the seventeenth century that both categories of play were seen together on the stage.

While the contemporary play deals with events taken from everyday life, it does not do so in the sense that it merely reproduces in the theater cozy domestic scenes. On the con-

32

trary, it is society's darker side that is the concern of the *sewamono*—its scandals, murders, and robberies. The famous "love-suicide" plays of Chikamatsu Monzaemon belong to this category. But whereas today plays dealing with such incidents might be considered of only passing interest, in the Edo period they were taken much more seriously. There was also a sense of urgency about them, the result of their having been often written at great speed, almost overnight. Thus it is said that Chikamatsu completed *Sonezaki Shinjū* (Love Suicides at Sonezaki) only one week after the actual event had taken place, adding the final touches while being rushed along in a palanquin. The fact that the Genroku era (1688–1704) produced so many masterpieces modeled on current events is proof of the great vitality and robustness of its culture.

From "Pure Contemporary" to "Cropped Hair" Plays

The Bunka-Bunsei era (1804–30) saw the advent of a variation on contemporary plays called *kizewamono* ("pure contemporary") plays. This genre, perfected by the playwright Tsuruya Namboku IV (1755–1829), is characterized by the realistic portrayal of life at the lower, poorer level of society.

The best example of this type of play is *Tōkaidō Yotsuya Kaidan* (Yotsuya Ghost Stories), which is regarded as a masterpiece for its depiction of the failures and misfits of life, particularly those of the *rōnin* (masterless warrior) class, of which the "hero," Iemon, is a member. When the play begins, Iemon is seen making paper umbrellas, the sort of work that masterless warriors were forced to engage in to survive. Inevitably, they would turn to crime to improve their lots. Iemon goes on to commit a number of murders and also conspires to poison his wife. For its portrayal of a callous villain, intent on success at any price, and its evocation of the decadent mood of the last days of the Edo period, *Tōkaidō Yotsuya Kaidan* is unrivaled in the Kabuki repertoire.

A new category of Kabuki play was created after the Meiji Restoration of 1868, when Japan began a process of rapid   33

Westernization. The "cropped hair" play (*zangirimono*) takes its name from the hairstyle of men during this period, who abandoned the traditional topknot in favor of the short back and sides of the West. The cropped hair play thus became the modern equivalent of the contemporary play of the Edo period, with many of the male characters dressed in suits, carrying gladstone bags, and sporting Western haircuts. But these plays only reflected the superficial changes in Japanese society. Despite their attempt to express the modern mood of the times, they were still performed according to traditional Kabuki conventions and the result was inevitable. Unable to abandon the traditions of the past, and with no progress in terms of dramaturgy, the cropped hair play failed to become the drama of the future and has largely been dropped from the repertoire.

Theatrical Conventions

An interesting convention of Kabuki in the past, one that lasted for more than 300 years, was that the New Year productions in Edo had to relate to the Soga brothers, heroes of the twelfth century remembered for the vendetta they carried to avenge their father's murder. In Kyoto and Osaka, however, the custom of the New Year was to present plays of the "courtesan" (*keiseimono*) variety.

The importance of the courtesan play in Kyoto and Osaka is hardly surprising. Kabuki began in that area and originally consisted of short dance-dramas portraying courtesans and their clients in the licensed quarter. The courtesan play is descended from this tradition, including the best surviving example, *Kuruwa Bunshō* (Love Letters from the Licensed Quarter). The important art of *wagoto* acting also derives from the courtesan play.

As for the Soga plays of Edo, it was the practice to write new ones every year. This also meant, of course, the creation of new titles, but the name "Soga" had to be included. Another convention related to the important "confrontation"

34

scene, when the brothers first come face to face with the man who killed their father. Whatever else a new Soga play contained, a confrontation scene was essential, and the point at which it occurred in the course of the play was also fixed by tradition. Much thought went into this meeting—the most important episode in the whole drama—and into how exactly it should take place between Soga no Gorō and Soga no Jūrō and Kudō Suketsune, the murderer of their father.

This approach to the writing of plays come to be regarded as nothing more than an example of the ceremonial and formal nature of Kabuki drama, the product of an intensely feudalistic society. But the urge to perform the same play or dance, again and again, is explained by the psychology behind it, for it is a kind of celebration and a source of joy and gratification to both spectators and participants. For this reason, of the Soga plays that have survived from the Edo period, it is the confrontation scene that remains the most popular and is still regularly performed.

This phenomenon of the annual staging of the same play at the New Year may seem strange enough. But even more so is the fact that it was not only the opening, historical play that had to be based upon the Soga brothers' vendetta, but the second, contemporary play as well. This practice was a peculiarity of Edo Kabuki, however. In Kyoto and Osaka it was not necessary for the first and second plays on the New Year program to have this kind of connection. In Edo, however, the situation became such that all the items on a day's program would be subtly connected by a single theme. Thus one hero in the contemporary play would be a transformation of someone who had previously been seen in the history play. A good example is that of Soga no Gorō, who would appear in the first play under his own name and in the appropriate historical setting. But in the second, contemporary play, he would appear under the assumed name of the contemporaneous hero Sukeroku, and be seen frequenting the Yoshiwara Licensed Quarter, which, of course, did not exist in the distant days of Soga no Gorō. Far from being discomfited by such inconsistencies and anachronisms, the Kabuki audiences of the past found them both amusing and sophisticated.

A similar situation exists regarding costumes in Kabuki. Despite a play's being set in a much earlier historical era, costume styles are likely to be those of the Edo period. Such incongruities are legion in Kabuki, but they are not the result of ignorance. Rather, they reflect the aesthetic values of the seventeenth and eighteenth centuries and also, as mentioned above, the influence of the law forbidding the portrayal of current events related to the ruling classes. This law, however, did not extend to the costumes, which explains the phenomenon, in the Edo period, of audiences delighting in the knowledge that, despite a historical setting, the plays they were watching dealt with recent events.

This illogical approach became unacceptable in the Meiji period, when rationalism was the prevailing intellectual trend, the result of Western influence. Accordingly, a new species of play came into existence, one that strove to be faithful to historical fact: the "living history" play (*katsurekigeki*). Yet for all its verisimilitude, the living history play lacked the pictorial quality of traditional Kabuki, the effect of gorgeous spectacle. Apart from occasional revivals, this type of play has all but disappeared from the repertoire.

Kabuki Dances and New Kabuki

In addition to the major categories of historical and contemporary plays, there is one more: that of dance.

Dances are of great importance in Kabuki and can be classified into two groups according to the two styles of vocalization that are fundamental to traditional Japanese music: the lyrical and the narrative. The difference between them is that, in the lyrical style, the words of the song have no particular story line or plot. In the narrative style, however, the element of storytelling is very strong.

The principal lyrical style of vocalization heard in Kabuki today is that of *nagauta* ("long song"), so called because a single piece consists of a number of *ko-uta* ("little songs")—popular ditties from the Edo period which attempt to capture in a few words a fleeting mood or emotion—which are strung loosely together to create a single, more substantial work. The majority of dances in the Kabuki repertoire are of the *nagauta* variety.

The narrative vocal style, *jōruri*, derives from the love story of Princess Jōruri and Ushiwakamaru, which enjoyed great popularity during the fifteenth century. There followed so many imitations that *jōruri* became their generic name. The three principal styles of *jōruri* are *gidayū*, *tokiwazu*, and *kiyomoto*, named after the men who created them in the seventeenth and eighteenth centuries.

The nineteenth century saw the creation of a new dance genre, the *hengemono* ("transformation" piece). This is a single long work consisting of a series of shorter dances all performed by the same dancer appearing in a number of different roles or transformations, young and old, male and female. One effect on Kabuki of this type of dance was that Kabuki actors became more versatile. Another was that dance itself became rather less the unique preserve of the female impersonator than it had formerly been.

During the Meiji period (1868–1912) a number of Noh and Kyōgen plays were successfully adapted to Kabuki as dance-dramas. Following to some degree the conventions of the originals, these dance-dramas are performed on the Kabuki version of the bare Noh stage with a simple backdrop of a single ancient pine tree (*matsu*). It is for this reason that much works are called *matsubame-mono*, two representative examples of which are *Tsuchigumo* (Earth Spider) and *Tsuri Onna* (Fishing for a Wife).

In the Edo period, Kabuki plays tended to be written by teams of playwrights who were permanent theater employees. According to this system, the principal playwright would decide on the plot and his assistants would each be assigned one act or section. While many masterpieces were created, a degree of stereotyping was inevitable. In the most blatant cases, playwrights would simply lift sections of previously performed plays and join them together to make new ones. Others specialized in reworking old plays to produce more polished versions, and many such works were staged.

In the twentieth century, however, Kabuki plays have been written by writers and dramatists with no professional connection whatsoever with the world of traditional drama. Such plays fall into the category of New Kabuki and strongly reflect Western influence. Despite this, a number have become modern "classics," including *Toribeyama Shinjū* (Love Suicides at Mt. Toribe) and *Shuzenji Monogatari* (The Tale of Shuzenji Temple), both by Okamoto Kidō (1872–1939).

MAKEUP, COSTUMES, AND ACTING

Kumadori Makeup

In the area of Kabuki acting there is a major difference between the traditional style of Edo, known as *aragoto*, and that of the Kyoto-Osaka region, a style known as *wagoto*.

Wagoto (literally, "soft [or 'gentle'] business") is the relatively realistic acting style associated with the handsome young lovers who are the heroes of the courtesan plays of Kabuki as it was performed in Kyoto and Osaka. Foppish and slightly effeminate, the *wagoto* hero is also something of a clown, even a spoiled child.

In complete contrast is the *aragoto* (literally, "rough [or 'violent'] business") style exemplified by the exaggerated posturing, costumes, and declamation of such martial heroes as Soga no Gorō and Kamakura Gongorō. The most obvious feature of *aragoto* is the makeup, *kumadori* (fig. 23), which involves the painting on the face of bold lines of principally red or blue in a way somewhat reminiscent of Peking Opera. *Kumadori* is also said to have been influenced by the expressions on the faces of Buddhist statues as well as by the masks used in Noh drama. The colors in *kumadori* have also taken on certain symbolic meanings so that, for example, red lines are likely to be associated with virtue or strength and blue with evil. Ghost and certain animal roles also involve the use of *kumadori* makeup.

23. *Shibaraku* (Wait!). Makeup (*kumadori*) of the villain Kiyohara no Takehira.

This remarkable type of makeup thus allowed character to be expressed directly and obviously in pictorial form. At the same time, however, it resulted in the stereotyping of roles into good and bad and the standardization of acting in Kabuki.

Wigs

Wigs are another remarkable aspect of Kabuki, one that has no exact equivalent in any other theatrical tradition in the world. What makes them so unusual is less their color—for Japanese hair is uniformly black—than their tremendous variety according to age, sex, and social class and status. In a Kabuki play, a change in wig that a particular character may be using is also intended to express a heightening of emotion as well as demonstrate psychological change. Thus, in the play *Narukami* (Narukami the Priest), for example, the actor in the principal role first appears in a wig having the hair combed back flat and smooth on the head in a style befitting a Buddhist sage endowed with supernatural powers (fig. 66). When Narukami reappears after his seduction by Princess Taema, however, his hair is literally standing on end, an indication of his corruption and rage (fig. 67). The wig used

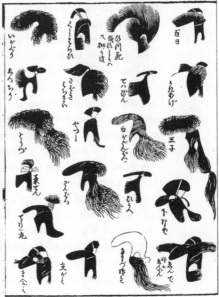

24. A selection of wigs for male (right) and female roles. From *Shibai Kimmō Zui* (Illustrated Encyclopedia of Kabuki), first published in 1803.

in this instance is called "one hundred days" (*hyakunichi*), a bushy mane representing one hundred days' growth of hair.

The contrast in the hairstyles of Narukami is achieved by a change of wigs offstage. With female characters, however, a similar transformation is achieved onstage, in full view of the audience. At the climactic moment, the actor will pull simultaneously on two side locks of hair, causing the rest to fall down over his shoulders. A characteristic Kabuki device, it is a most effective way of revealing to the audience the extent of a woman's jealousy and anger.

Onstage Costume Transformation

Not only wigs but also costumes can undergo a sudden onstage transformation during the course of a play or dance. Again, 41 this is a phenomenon not to be found in any other type of drama in the world. These transformations take place in full view of the audience and are of two types: *hikinuki* and *bukkaeri*.

In the case of *hikinuki* (or "pull-out"; fig. 25), the upper and lower sections of the actor's kimono are separate, but this is hidden by the wide sash. At the appropriate moment, threads are pulled from the sleeves and skirts, loosening the top and bottom halves of the outer kimono, which can then be removed at great speed from the sash to reveal, in an instant, a new kimono beneath.

A good example of the use of *hikinuki* is in the dance *Musume Dōjōji* (The Maiden at Dōjōji Temple), in which the dancer in the principal role first appears wearing a scarlet kimono decorated with a motif of hanging cherry blossoms. At the conclusion of a sequence involving the miming of a little girl bouncing a ball, the scarlet kimono is removed by the *hikinuki* technique to reveal one of pale green beneath. The cherry blossom pattern, however, is the same. In other words, the

25. *Sagi Musume.* An onstage costume change (*hikinuki*, or "pull-out"), in which the entire outer layer of kimono is removed to reveal another beneath.

color of the kimono changes, but not the design. This phenomenon relates to Kabuki as it was in the Edo period, when performances at night were prohibited. As Kabuki was only performed between dawn and dark, little progress was made as far as lighting effects were concerned. This deficiency was compensated for, to some extent, by such methods as the *hikinuki*, which produced the kind of effects that could only otherwise have been achieved by sophisticated lighting.

The technique of *hikinuki* is a difficult one requiring great skill on the part of the stage assistants who carry it out. In the case of *Musume Dōjōji*, the threads of the kimono must be pulled out discreetly and efficiently from behind as the dancer turns first one side of his body, then the other, away from the audience. Unless the movements of both assistants and actor are perfectly timed, the spectacular effect of the sudden removal of the outer kimono will not be achieved.

The other technique, *bukkaeri* (or "flip-down"), does not involve the complete removal of the outer costume. Instead, threads are removed from the shoulders and sleeves only, so that the front and rear panels of the upper garment come away and hang down like skirts to create a new costume with a new color and design. *Bukkaeri* can be seen at the end of *Musume Dōjōji*, when the maiden finally reveals her true form, that of a serpent, and also in *Narukami*. In the latter, the loss of the priest's spiritual purity following his seduction, and his metamorphosis into a fiend, is demonstrated visually by the transformation of his plain white robe into one decorated with a design of orange flames (figs. 3, 67). *Bukkaeri*, therefore, is used to symbolize a change of personality, the revelation of one's real nature. *Hikinuki*, however, is only used for its visual appeal.

Characteristics of Kabuki Acting

Acting varies according to the type of play. This means that the acting in historical plays will be extremely stylized, that in contemporary drama relatively realistic. (The "rough" 43 *aragoto* and "soft" *wagoto* styles are important in this connection and are discussed on page 50.) Some plays, however, combine both. In *Aoto Zōshi Hana no Nishiki-e* (The Gang of Five), the young thief, Benten Kozō, who has previously been speaking in the contemporary style, changes to that of the historical play for the famous speech in which he reveals his true identity and announces his real name for all to hear. This change in his tone of voice and manner of delivery is both impressive and effective, but only so long as such stylization is accepted as natural and essential to Kabuki. If not, Kabuki will only appear foolish and insipid.

Another Kabuki characteristic is what has been described as "staggered" or "sequential" acting. An example of this is the phenomenon of characters in historical plays not *immediately* breaking down and weeping no matter how tragic or pathetic a scene may be. This means that the acting is not synchronized to the words, neither the actor's nor those of the narrator. Instead, it is only *after* the narrator, in a historical play, has informed the audience that a certain character in the play is about to weep that the actor in the role will actually do so with the appropriate gestures and sounds.

As for contemporary plays, these require a more realistic approach than historical plays, but there are still certain conventions and patterns of acting that must be adhered to. Murders and fight scenes, for example, which would look quite gruesome if presented realistically, are invariably highly stylized. Those occurring in dances and dance-dramas, in particular, are executed to a complex choreography.

Stylized Entries and Exits

Another feature of the Kabuki actor's art of movement is the *roppō*, according to which an exit is performed along the *hanamichi* in a series of leaps and bounds.

The literal meaning of *roppō* is "six directions," but there are various opinions as to the real significance of this curious term. One theory has it that the actor's hands and feet ac-

26. *Kanjinchō*. Benkei's "one-armed" *roppō* at the end of the play.

27. *Yoshitsune Sembon Zakura*, act 4, scene 1, "The Journey to Mt. Yoshino." The "fox" *roppō* of Tadanobu.

tually move in six directions. Another is that the *roppō* derives from the unusual posture and gait or the *roppō-gumi* ("*roppō* gangs"), bands of ruffians who were common in Edo at the end of the seventeenth century. A third traces the term to *roppō-shū* ("*roppō* associations"), a class of low-ranking priests who practiced an arrogant strut. Whichever is correct, the *roppō* now exists in various forms (figs. 26, 27): the *kitsune* (fox) *roppō*, the *oyogi* (swimming) *roppō*, the *katate* (one-armed) *roppō*, etc.

The *tanzen* can also be thought of as a type of *roppō* except that, strictly speaking, the latter is performed along the *hana-michi* as an exit, whereas the former is likely to occur during an actor's entrance on the *hanamichi*, as in *Sukeroku Yukari no Edo Zakura* (Sukeroku, Flower of Edo). The word *tanzen* is said to derive from the gait of the young men who frequented a certain public bathhouse in Edo in the middle of the seventeenth century.

Mie Poses

The term *mie* refers to the pose that is one of the most remarkable features of Kabuki and which is most likely to occur at a climactic movement in a play or dance. The action comes to a temporary halt as the actor assumes a fixed pose, making, as he does so, a rotating, nodding movement of the head and crossing one eye (fig. 28). The *mie* pose is invariably performed to the beating of two wooden blocks on a board at the side of the stage.

Nori Speeches

At points of heightened emotion during a historical play, a speech may sometimes be delivered in a markedly rhythmic fashion timed to the accompaniment of the (*takemoto*) shamisen. Called *nori* (literally, "riding [the shamisen strings]"), this style of delivery is invariably adopted by messengers who arrive to report on the progress or outcome of a battle. At such times the movements of the actor may be very pronounced, verging on dance.

"Divided" and "Passed-Along" Speeches

A peculiarity of Kabuki is that a single speech may be shared by a number of actors, each of whom speaks a part of the whole. If only two or three actors are involved, this is referred to as "divided" speech (*wari-zerifu*). If more actors are involved—each one speaking in turn as if part of a chain—the term "passed-along speech" (*watari-zerifu*) is used.

A good example of the *watari-zerifu* occurs in act 4 of *Imoseyama Onna Teikin* (Exemplary Tales for Women) when a group of ladies-in-waiting delivers one fragment each of a long speech, with the last part spoken in chorus. Which actor speaks which section is less important than the delivery of the whole speech in the correct order, an approach unthinkable in Western drama, in which it is precisely through the spoken lines that the nature of an actor's role is revealed and expressed. In this respect, Kabuki shows itself to be essentially musical drama, for in many cases what is said is less important than the delivery, which, timed to the accompanying music, should be rhythmical and easy on the ear.

28. *Shibaraku* (Wait!). A "Genroku" *mie* pose.   47

THE
ACTORS

Role Specialization and Artistic Transmission

No other Japanese theatrical art displays the role-specialization
found in Kabuki. This is true even today, when strictures are
less binding than in the past. Broadly speaking, Kabuki roles
can be divided into male and female, both of which are played
by men. Traditionally, actors of male roles are known as
tachiyaku; those of female roles as *oyama*. The word *tachiyaku*
literally means "one whose role is to stand [and dance]," and
was intended to distinguish the actors from the musicians,
who performed while seated. With the advent of the female
impersonator, *tachiyaku* came to designate either male-role actors as a whole or the actors of the leading male roles.

The word *oyama* that now designates a female impersonator
referred originally to a courtesan in the Osaka-Kyoto region.
Since the portrayal of these courtesans marked the high point
of an actor's career, the word became a synonym for the actors of such roles, and eventually for female impersonators
in general. The word is thought pejorative, however, so that
the more neutral *onnagata* is often preferred. There is also
another term available for use: "mezzanine," or *chūnikai*. As
strange as this term may appear, the story behind it is quite
simple. In Edo, buildings of more than three stories were prohibited by law, because of the danger from earthquakes and
fire. In fact, however, Kabuki theaters were three-story struc-
tures, but circumvented the proscription by referring eu-

phemistically to the second story as the mezzanine. It was here that the dressing rooms of the female impersonators were found, leading eventually to an identification of locus and role.

The existence of the female impersonator in Kabuki is without parallel in any other mature theatrical tradition. It is true that female impersonators were once found in Peking Opera, but they have gradually been replaced by actresses, leaving Kabuki the sole theatrical form in the world in which the female impersonator is a *sine qua non*. The phenomenon of actors playing female roles in Kabuki dates from 1629, when women were officially banned from the stage. In this connection it is argued in certain quarters that the female impersonator is a remnant from the feudal past, that the institution should be scrapped and actresses introduced instead. This argument is naive and unacceptable. The presence of actresses on the Kabuki stage would constitute a denial of the entire artistic history of Kabuki from the time of the first female impersonator to the present day. The uprooting of the art and mystique of the *oyama* would mean a radical transmutation of aesthetic and artistic values nurtured over three hundred years.

Not only does role specialization find meaning in Kabuki, but without it Kabuki itself is devoid of meaning. In other words, Kabuki is a drama of stylization, and it is essential that its acting styles and conventions be transmitted from one generation of actors to the next. In order to appreciate the nature of the problem, it is necessary to consider the question of family lineage.

Historically, great emphasis has always been placed on the type of roles that a particular family of actors has made its specialty. For it is through these families that the actor's art was passed on, either to a direct blood descendant, to an adopted child, or, in some cases, to a chosen pupil (who assumes the family name). Thus, when an actor succeeds to a new name, he also inherits the acting traditions connected with it as well as the responsibility of maintaining them. Such 49 traditions are seen, for instance, in the Ichikawa Danjūrō line, which specializes in the style known as "rough business" (*aragoto*); in the Sawamura Sōjūrō line and its "soft business" (*wagoto*) style; and in the Onoe family with its tradition of performing ghost plays. Furthermore, different lineages have different interpretations of the same role. Accordingly, one actor's treatment of the role of Kumagai in *Ichinotani Futaba Gunki* (Chronicle of the Battle of Ichinotani) or of Kampei in *Kanadehon Chūshingura* (The Treasury of Loyal Retainers) will depend on the line of actors to which he belongs and will differ from that of another actor following another tradition.

In addition, complete plays may be associated with one particular line or family. The *kabuki jūhachiban* (Kabuki Eighteen), for example, is a group of eighteen plays long connected with the Ichikawa Danjūrō line. As a collection, they exemplify the "rough" style of acting, a specialty of the Danjūrō line. Individually, they not only exist as Kabuki plays in their own right, but are likely to be performed by actors not necessarily connected with the Danjūrō line.

As has been demonstrated, when an actor inherits the name of an esteemed predecessor, he also inherits certain conventions and traditions which he must maintain in order to prove his worth. At the same time, however, he must give an individual stamp to the roles he undertakes. As a result, the Kabuki actor has a double burden to bear: to continue the traditions of the past and, at the same time, to give the fullest demonstration of his own capabilities as an artist.

From Troupe Head to Walk-on Player

Rank, in the world of Kabuki, is stressed to an almost inordinate degree. This is evident in the troupe, or *za*, which is a more or less fixed gathering of actors from different families for the performance of plays. The following discussion is chiefly applicable to the troupe in its traditional form, and only marginally to present-day conditions, which have undergone 50 considerable change.

29. Low-ranking actors in their communal dressing room. From *Shibai Kimmō Zui* (Illustrated Encyclopedia of Kabuki), first published in 1803.

The position of leader of the troupe, or "troupe head" (*zagashira*), is monopolized by the principal actor of leading male roles. He controls everything from administration, personnel, and backstage arrangements to the allocation of roles and the direction of plays. The principal actor of female roles, the *tate-oyama*, is aligned with the troupe head at the top of the organization and is responsible for the overall supervision and instruction of the female impersonators.

Actors of sufficient rank to warrant the display of their names outside the theater are called *nadai* ("billboard"). Those who do not are known as *nadai shita* ("below the rank of *nadai*"). Subordinate to this group are the *shita tachiyaku* (lowest rank of male-role actor), at which level those who enter Kabuki with no family connection must begin their careers (fig. 29). The duties of such subordinate actors include the performance of walk-on and similar parts and, if necessary, animal roles (figs. 30, 31).

30–31. Walk-on actors are
also required to perform the
various animal roles that are
frequently found in Kabuki.
From *Shibai Kimmō Zui* (Illustrated Encyclopedia of Kabuki), first published in 1803.

As well as indicating rank, the theater billboard also con-
tributed to the naming of certain roles. For example, actors
of romantic male roles were listed in the second row (*nimai-
me*) on the bill. This led to their being referred to as "second
row," which, in common parlance, has come to mean any
handsome young man. In the same way, the names of actors
of comic roles were always listed in the third row (*sanmai-me*),
and that term is now synonymous with clown.

Actors' Official and Actual Status
Kabuki actors went on to achieve such popularity in the Edo
period that the only modern parallel is with the mania surrounding film and rock stars. After all, in those days neither

52

the cinema nor television existed, and Kabuki was the only live contemporary theater. The actor Ichikawa Yaozō II, for example, was so idolized, between the years 1760 and 1780, that when he performed the role of Sukeroku—which required him to submerge himself in a barrel of real water—the water was afterward bottled and sold to hordes of adoring female fans. Similarly, when Ichikawa Danjūrō VIII committed suicide in 1854, at the age of thirty-two, more than 500 different woodblock portraits were created in commemoration, from each of which hundreds of impressions were made and sold.

Given this adulation, it was only natural that the incomes of the more popular actors were considerable. In fact, despite government attempts to regulate them, the private lives of some actors were said to rival that of a feudal lord in comfort and extravagance. Ichimura Uzaemon XII (1812–51), for example, presided over sumptuous private parties at which were served fresh fish from his own fishery. And when visiting a hot spring or going on an excursion into the mountains, he was invariably accompanied by an entourage of forty people or more, including musicians, jesters, geisha, property men, and hairdressers. In the case of Ichikawa Danjūrō VII (1791–1859), the luxury in which he lived was such that the government felt obliged to exile him from Edo as punishment.

For all this, Kabuki actors belonged officially to the lowest social class—that of the outcasts—and were contemptuously referred to as "riverbed beggars" (kawara kojiki) and "hut people" (koyamono). The law even required them to live and work within the confines of the theater district, venturing out only under large sedge hats that concealed their features. It was only after the Meiji Restoration of 1868 that discrimination was abolished and actors were able to take their first steps both as legitimate stage artists and as guardians of the traditions of Kabuki. For by that time Kabuki was no longer the representative theater of the people but a classical dramatic art rooted in the past.

COLOR
AND
MUSIC

The Colors of Kabuki

Kabuki expresses itself in strong, basic colors such as red, black, and green, not in the sober and restrained hues of classical Japanese art. Indeed it is no exaggeration to say that Kabuki positively delights in violent clashes of brilliant, even vulgar colors, in a way seemingly at odds with the refinement and elegance usually held up as the ideal of traditional aristocratic taste. That this conception of beauty was the creation of the townsmen of the Edo period is a phenomenon often ignored by many who dilate on Japanese aesthetics.

Kabuki evolved together with the art of the woodblock print and also with the modish fashions of the day, in all of which color played a conspicuous role. It should also be borne in mind that, in an age that was extremely backward in methods of artificial lighting, it is for that reason, perhaps, that it was correspondingly advanced in its use of rich and vivid color schemes. In Kabuki, where modern lighting was lacking and performances restricted to the hours of daylight, color was exploited for maximum effect by methods that were remarkably sophisticated. Two obvious examples are the *bukkaeri* and *hikinuki* techniques mentioned above, by means of which changes in costume colors can be instantaneously achieved. Another is that of makeup, particularly the type known as *kumadori*, in which bold and brilliant colors are used not only for their visual appeal but also as a clue to the nature of the character portrayed.

It is in historical plays, however, that the richest and most sumptuous colors are most in evidence, not only in the costumes and makeup but particularly in the scenery and settings. Especially impressive are the gold and vermilion temples and palaces that rise into view on a trap lift, or a great gate surrounded by a landscape of cherry blossoms, upon which an arch-villain or thief is likely to be installed, smoking a pipe and admiring the view. In contrast to the visual splendors of historical plays, the colors seen in contemporary (*sewamono*) dramas are relatively subdued.

The Sounds of Kabuki

The sounds of Kabuki can be called ''aural colors,'' those that appeal not to the eye but to the ear. As for Kabuki music,

32. Musicians relaxing backstage. From *Shibai Kimmō Zui* (Illustrated Encyclopedia of Kabuki), first published in 1803.

it is known as *hayashi*, and can be broadly divided into two main categories: *debayashi*, which is music performed onstage, in full view of the audience; and *kagebayashi*, which is performed offstage, out of sight. The onstage musicians are situated either at the back of the stage on a dais of red felt or at one or other of the stage's two sides (occasionally both). Their instruments, generally speaking, consist of shamisens, drums, and a flute (in the lyrical or *nagauta* style) or shamisens alone (in the narrative or *jōruri* style), with the addition in both cases of singers. The offstage variety of music is performed behind the black latticed screen (called *kuromisu*) of a small room situated at the left of the stage as seen from the audience. For this reason, this type of music is called *kuromisu* (or *geza*) music and, together with singers, consists of musicians who play not only the shamisen but also a whole range of percussion and other instruments, including drums, bells, gongs, and flutes. These are used to perform hundreds of accompanying melodies and themes that have become more or less fixed by custom and tradition, everything from ceremonial court music to lively festival tunes. Its tremendous variety is perhaps the most remarkable feature of *kuromisu* music.

In Kabuki, sounds are also used to achieve the kinds of effects that are created visually in other forms of drama. The large drum, for example, can be struck in various ways to evoke rain, wind, a rushing river, or ocean waves. Even the soundless sound of falling snow can be effectively conveyed. This and other sound effects have a hallucinatory quality that excites the audience's interest. Again, the emergence of a ghost is accompanied by the wailing of a flute and a dry rattle on the large drum.

A sound fundamental to Kabuki is that of the *hyōshigi*: two wooden blocks that are struck together at increasing speed as the curtain is run open or shut at the beginning or conclusion of a scene. An art in itself, the striking of the *hyōshigi* is an important staging convention, one of the best examples of which occurs at the start of the play *Kanadehon Chūshingura*

(The Treasury of Loyal Retainers). Because the number of retainers is forty-seven, the *hyōshigi* are struck forty-seven times as the curtain slowly opens at the beginning of act 1.

Another type of *hyōshigi* are those struck not together but downward against a board placed on the floor of the stage at the far right of the stage as seen from the audience. This is done in a variety of rhythmic patterns to accompany fight scenes, a rapid entry or exit along the *hanamichi*, or, most important of all, to accentuate the *mie* poses of the leading actors.

The most characteristic, indeed indispensable, sound in Kabuki, however, is that of the shamisen, a three-stringed instrument plucked with a large ivory plectrum. Introduced into Japan via China and Okinawa, the shamisen provides the basic accompaniment to Kabuki, sometimes a romantic, even sensuous atmosphere.

All in all, it can be said that the Kabuki resembles the musical of the West in certain ways. In that respect, therefore, the role of music in Kabuki is quite as important as that of color.

THIRTY-SIX
PLAYS:
Synopses and Highlights

[Since the English titles of Kabuki plays are variously translated and thus unreliable as a means of reference, the synopses below are alphabetically listed according to the Japanese titles. These are given in their standard forms except for dances, the titles of which have been abbreviated. An alphabetical listing of English titles used in this book, together with their Japanese counterparts, is given on page 143.]

33. The program having been drawn up, the names and roles of the revelant actors are declaimed before the theater. From *Shibai Kimmō Zui* (Illustrated Encyclopedia of Kabuki, first published in 1803.

Aoto Zōshi Hana no Nishiki-e (The Gang of Five)

A masterpiece by Kawatake Mokuami (1816–93), who is often called the "thieves' dramatist" for the many plays he wrote about thieves and villains. Mokuami was active at the end of the Edo period, and his works (including this "contemporary" [_sewamono_] piece, which is one of the best examples) often reflect the prevailing mood of decadence and corruption. _Aoto Zōshi Hana no Nishiki-e_ was first staged in 1862. Originally in five acts, acts 3 and 4 are the most frequently performed today, although act 5 may occasionally be seen.

Act 3, "The Hamamatsuya Kimono Store"

Benten Kozō Kikunosuke is a member of a gang of thieves led by the notorious Nippon Daemon. Benten and Nangō Rikimaru, another member of the gang, respectively disguise themselves as the daughter of an important samurai and her retainer. Together they go to the Hamamatsuya kimono store, pretending to be shopping for the girl's dowry. As he examines various materials, Benten slips among them a piece of cloth, but then picks it up again and hides it ostentatiously inside his kimono. Accused of shoplifting, Benten Kozō is struck on the head with a wooden abacus by the chief clerk. But when he produces evidence to prove that the cloth was brought at another shop, the clerks apologize and Nangō demands a large sum of money in compensation.

At that moment they are interrupted by a samurai, Tamashima Ittō (actually Nippon Daemon), who denounces Benten and Nangō as extortionists. Furthermore, he also claims that Benten Kozō is a man dressed as a woman (fig. 8). All of this is part of the gang's larger strategy. In the climax to the scene, Benten sits cross-legged on the floor and announces who he really is. Slipping his left arm and shoulder from his kimono, he reveals a tattoo with a cherry blossom design (fig. 34). The change in Benten's behavior and speech, from refined young lady to sneering delinquent, is the principal point of interest.

Act 4, "Inase River"

Pursued by the police to the banks of the river, the five thieves   59

34–36. *Aoto Zōshi Hana no Nishiki-e*, act 3 (right), "The Hamamatsuya Kimono Store." Benten Kozō at the conclusion of his famous speech in which he reveals his true identity. Act 4 (below), "Inase River." Dressed in magnificent kimonos, the members of the gang assemble by the river where they make florid speeches of self-introduction in defiance of the police arranged behind. Act 5 (bottom), scene 1, "The Roof of the Gokurakuji Temple." Benten Kozō commits ritual suicide on the roof of the temple, which then rotates backward as the main gate begins to rise into view on the trap lift below.

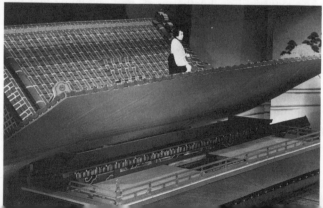

line up on the *hanamichi* dressed in brilliantly colored kimonos. Costumes, music, and *mie* poses all add to the total effect as the five thieves proceed to the main stage, where one by one they make flowery speeches of self-introduction. The police surround them, and amid the blossoming cherry trees along the bank of the river, the thieves pose with their umbrellas (fig. 35).

Act 5, scene 1, "The Roof of the Gokurakuji Temple"
Benten Kozō escapes to the roof of the Gokurakuji temple, where he fights off the police trying to arrest him. Finally, he commits suicide by self-disembowelment, and in an impressive change of scenery the roof of the temple rotates backward (fig. 36) and out of sight as the main gate rises into view on a trap lift.

Act 5, scene 2, "The Gate of the Temple"
Nippon Daemon is revealed on top of the gate. Dressed in a manner befitting an arch-criminal of Kabuki, he wears a heavy padded outer kimono and a bushy "hundred days" wig. The chief of police, Aoto Saemon, then appears, and after a lively exchange of words Daemon offers to surrender.

Dammari (Dumb Show)

Dammari, which means "pantomime" or "dumb show," is not the title of a play but the name of an important performing style. A "dumb-show" scene usually occurs during the course of a longer play, as a means of presenting the principal members of the cast assembled together for the first time.

In its basic form the "dumb show" is conventionally set in some lonely spot, such as a forest, where the characters appear in a variety of different guises: a warrior, a thief, a footman, a princess, and suchlike. As the scene is meant to be taking place in total darkness, the participants move slowly, feeling their way about the stage. Eventually the doors of a wooden wayside shrine open and the leading actor appears in the guise of an arch-villain or thief wearing an impressive "hundred days" wig (fig. 37). Having performed several "pillar-wrapping" *mie* poses, in the past the prerogative of the troupe leader, he makes his way to   61

37. *Dammari*. In a variety of typical Kabuki roles and
costumes, the actors arrange themselves for a final tableau.

the foot of the *hanamichi*. Meanwhile the outer costumes of the
rest of the cast are removed (by the "pull-out" [*hikinuki*] technique) to reveal more brilliant and impressive ones beneath.
All arrange themselves for a final *mie* pose as the curtain is
closed, leaving the troupe leader to perform a dynamic "six-
directions" (*roppō*) exit along the *hanamichi*.

Many "dumb-show" scenes (e.g., *Miyajima Dammari* and
Kuramayama Dammari) are now performed independently. Originally, however, they were part of a much longer "historical" (*jidaimono*) play, which was staged at the annual "face-
showing" (*kao-mise*) performance that took place in November
in the Edo period, the traditional beginning of the new theatrical year. A "dumb-show" scene was the most effective way of
introducing to the theater's patrons the actors who had been
engaged by a theater for the next twelve months.

"Dumb-show" scenes occur not only in "historical" plays but
in "contemporary" (*sewamono*) pieces as well. Being an integral
part of the plays for which they were written, they are never performed independently. Nevertheless, such scenes still have a
distinctive atmosphere of their own. Often they involve a small
stage property, like a wallet or letter. Essential to the subsequent
development of the plot, this article is likely to be found accidentally on the ground and picked up by one of the characters, who

will examine it by the light of a lantern. Another device, common in "contemporary dumb-shows" (*sewa-dammari*), is that of a sleeve being torn off in a struggle and left in the hand of the would-be captor, who then watches his intended victim escape along the *hanamichi*.

Performed in silence, except for the accompanying music, the "dumb show" is designed to show off the art of the actors involved as well as the beauty of the costumes. Simple but highly effective, it can be enjoyed as pure Kabuki, that is, as something unique to the art uninfluenced by any outside form like Bunraku or Noh. The experience of watching a "dumb-show" scene has been compared to that of viewing Kabuki "through the glass walls of an aquarium."

Ehon Taikōki (Chronicle of the Last Days of Mitsuhide)

Written by Chikamatsu Yanagi and others, this "historical" (*jidaimono*) piece was first staged as a play for puppets in 1799. Originally in thirteen acts, only act 10 is now normally performed.

This work is based upon the revolt of Akechi Mitsuhide, which took place in June, 1582. The period of Mitsuhide's rise and fall was only thirteen days, from June 1, when he raised his rebellion, to June 13, when he was defeated and killed. In accordance with Kabuki convention, the name of the hero has been changed to Takechi Mitsuhide.

Act 10, "The Retreat at Amagasaki"

Mitsuhide's mother, Satsuki, disapproving of her son's rebellion, has gone to live in retreat in the country. Satsuki is visited by Mitsuhide's wife, Misao, as well as by Hatsugiku, the betrothed of Mitsuhide's son, Jūjirō. Satsuki also gives a night's lodging to a mendicant priest asking for shelter.

Jūjirō himself arrives in order to say farewell before his departure for the front. Mitsuhide then emerges from a bamboo grove behind the trellis. Dressed in armor and wearing a straw cloak to keep off the rain, he hides his face behind a sedge   63 hat. Having realized that the mendicant priest is his enemy Hisayoshi in disguise, Mitsuhide stealthily approaches the house. Cutting himself a bamboo spear, he thrusts it through the paper-covered sliding doors of the house, intending to kill Hisayoshi, but it is his mother, Satsuki, whom he stabs.

The dying Satsuki admonishes her son for his rebellious ways, and Misao also pleads with him, but to no avail. If that were not enough, his son Jūjirō returns from the battlefield mortally wounded.

Jūjirō describes how his father's troops have been defeated, gradually weakening as he does so. Fading fast, and almost blind, Jūjirō tries desperately to make out the face of Hatsugiku. Jūjirō and Satsuki die, and Mitsuhide is so overcome that he breaks down and weeps.

Surveying the surrounding countryside, Mitsuhide sees his forces in retreat from those of Hisayoshi, who appears at that moment. The play comes to an end as the two agree to meet once again on the battlefield (fig. 38).

38. *Ehon Taikōki*, act 10, ''The Retreat at Amagasaki.'' Mitsuhide (left) and Hisayoshi agree to meet once again on the battlefield.

Fuji Musume (The Wisteria Maiden)

Now performed independently to lyrical (*nagauta*) music, *Fuji Musume* was first staged in 1826 as one of a set of five dances. Each dance represented a figure come to life from a type of picture known as *ōtsu-e*, which was a popular souvenir among travelers to the town of Ōtsu on Lake Biwa, near Kyoto. One of the best-known *ōtsu-e* pictures was that of young girl wearing a black lacquer hat and holding a branch of wisteria blossoms over one shoulder. This dance is based on that image, but a more recent interpretation is that the girl is the spirit of the wisteria in human form (fig. 39).

Fuji Musume proceeds in a series of sections depicting the girl at play, falling in love, and becoming slightly tipsy from too much sake. A charming and picturesque dance, it has recently become extremely popular and is frequently performed.

39. *Fuji Musume*. The spirit of the wisteria, in the shape of a young girl, dances beneath the wisteria vines.

Futa Omote (Double Possession)

First performed in 1775, this dance-drama was originally part of a longer play in which the reprobate priest Hōkaibō is enamored of Okumi, a merchant's daughter, who is herself in love with a clerk in her father's shop. The clerk turns out to be Matsuwaka, a young nobleman who has disguised himself as a   65

40. *Futa Omote*. Okumi (left) and her lover, Matsukawa (right),
are tormented by Okumi's double, actually the malignant spirits
of the dead Hōkaibō and Nowake, which have combined and
taken the shape of a single human being.

commoner in order to retrieve a lost family heirloom.

Matsuwaka's betrothed, Nowake, comes to visit him, but she
is murdered by Hōkaibō, who has joined forces with the young
man's enemies. Nowake dies bearing a grudge against Okumi,
as does Hōkaibō when he, too, is eventually killed.

Bearing baskets of flowers, Okumi and Matsuwaka come to
the banks of the river Sumida where they meet Oshizu, a woman
in charge of the ferry boat, and lament the death of Nowake.
As they offer their prayers, a girl mysteriously appears, the exact double of Okumi. Matsuwaka is at first confused, but the
double turns out to be the malignant spirits of Hōkaibō and
Nowake, which have combined and metamorphosed themselves
into the shape of Okumi (fig. 40). Sticking out its tongue and
extending an arm, the ghost torments the two in various ways
but is eventually subdued by a statue of Kannon, the Buddhist
goddess of mercy, which the ferry woman produces.

This dance is a good example of a common Kabuki theme,
that of two malevolent spirits who, bearing a grudge against the
same person, combine to manifest themselves in the shape of
that person and create confusion in the real world. The actor
in the role of the second Okumi must make it clear from his
movements that one side of his body is inhabited by Hōkaibō,
the other by Nowake.

Gempei Nunobiki no Taki (The Nunobiki Waterfall)

A "historical" (*jidaimono*) drama based upon episodes from the Heike-Genji wars, it was written by Namiki Senryū and Miyoshi Shōraku for the Bunraku theater. First performed in 1749, the original play is in five acts, but now only act 3 is regularly staged and popularly known as *Sanemori Monogatari* (The Recitation of Sanemori), after the famous speech of the hero that is the climax.

Act 3, "The House of Kurosuke"

The background to this scene is as follows: The Genji general Minamoto no Yoshikata has recently been defeated and killed when his mansion was attacked by Heike troops. Before his death, Yoshikata gave the precious white banner of the Genji clan to Koman, the adopted daughter of Kurosuke, a farmer loyal to the Genji, with strict instructions not to let it fall into enemy hands. In order to escape the Heike troops, Koman jumped into Lake Biwa and desperately swam away. In this act, Yoshikata's pregnant widow, Lady Aoi, is being sheltered by Kurosuke at his house. Kurosuke and Tarokichi, Koman's small son, who have been fishing in the lake, return home with a human arm that got caught in their net—the hand of which is clutching a white banner.

Meanwhile the Heike are anxious to capture any survivors of their recent attack on Yoshikata's mansion—particularly Yoshikata's widow, Aoi. As Kurosuke and the others are anxiously examining the arm, two Heike warriors, Saitō Sanemori and Senō Jūrō, arrive in search of Aoi, whom they know to be hiding there. The two have been ordered to kill all Genji males, even infants, and Senō threatens to cut open Aoi to examine the child she is carrying.

In a ruse to save Aoi, Kurosuke's wife, Oyoshi, pretends that Aoi has gone into labor and leaves to assist her. Later she returns with a bundle, but it turns out to contain not a baby but the arm from the lake. Oyoshi claims that Aoi gave birth to the arm, but Senō angrily refuses to believe it. Sanemori, who once fought on the Genji side and remains secretly loyal, is anxious to pro-

67

41. *Gempei Nunobiki no Taki*, act 3, "The House of Kurosuke." Sanemori poses on horseback before making his exit along the *hanamichi*.

tect Aoi from Senō. Sanemori supports the old woman's claim and cites an ancient Chinese legend about a similar unnatural birth. Senō announces that he will go and report the matter to Kiyomori, the leader of the Heike clan. But, once outside, Senō hides at the back of the house to spy.

Aoi, still pregnant, enters and thanks Sanemori for saving her. In a famous "recitation" (*monogatari*), Sanemori explains that he had earlier been feasting with Kiyomori in a ship on Lake Biwa. While doing so, he noticed a woman in the water and rescued her. She turned out to be Koman, carrying the Genji banner. Because of his secret loyalty to the Genji clan, Sanemori was anxious to prevent the banner from falling into Kiyomori's hands. For that reason, Sanemori cut off Koman's arm so that it dropped into the water together with the banner. Koman herself was then thrown back into the lake.

The others are distraught at the news that the arm is that of Koman, and Tarokichi, her son, calls Sanemori a murderer and, child though he is, threatens to kill him. At that moment, however, the body of Koman is brought in and Sanemori places the arm beside it. All begin to pray, and the arm is miraculously restored to the body and Koman revives long enough for her to be satisfied that the Genji banner is now safe. The shock of all this is too much for Aoi, who goes into labor and produces a son, of whom Tarokichi is made the retainer.

Having observed all this from his hiding place, Senō realizes that Koman is his daughter, whom he abandoned as a child. Anxious to help Tarokichi, his grandson, win his spurs as a warrior, Senō provokes the boy into wounding him, and then allows the boy to behead him. Tarokichi then wishes to avenge his mother's, Koman's, death by killing Sanemori. But Sanemori tells the boy he must wait until he is a full-grown man, at which time he promises to meet him on the battlefield. Sanemori then mounts his horse and departs (fig. 41).

As well as Sanemori's "recitation" (*monogatari*), after which the scene is named when staged independently, much of the interest lies in the contrast between the chivalrous hero and the apparently villainous Senō. To emphasize the contrast, Sanemori wears white makeup and Senō red.

Hiragana Seisuiki (A Simple Chronicle of the Vicissitudes of the Heike and Genji Clans)

This "historical" (*jidaimono*) play was written for the Bunraku theater by Takeda Izumo II and others and first performed in 1739. A dramatization of the medieval chronicle *Gempei Seisuiki* (Chronicle of the Vicissitudes of the Genji and Heike Clans), it is set against the background of the wars between the two clans from the death of Kiso Yoshinaka, in 1184, to the battle of Ichinotani later in the same year. More specifically, it deals with the rivalry on the battlefield between Kajiwara Genta and Sasaki Takatsuna; the attempt by Higuchi no Jirō to avenge the death of his lord, Kiso Yoshinaka; and the legend of the bell of a certain Kannon Temple, according to which anyone striking it would be granted a wish, but go to hell as a result. At present, only acts 2 and 3 are usually performed, and act 4 rarely.

Act 2, "The Disowning of Genta"
The Genji general Kajiwara Kagetoki is taking part in a battle against Kiso Yoshinaka, the leader of a rival faction within the 69

same clan. Kagetoki's son, Genta, is also involved in the fighting. Genta's younger brother, Heiji, feigns illness and remains at home, where he spends most of his time pursuing Chidori, Genta's betrothed, of whom he is enamored.

Genta returns to the mansion, sent home in disgrace by his father for having failed to win the honor of being first to cross the Uji River and engage the enemy. In what is the climax to this part of the play, Genta describes the circumstances of the battle in answer to questions from his anxious family.

By rights, Genta should commit suicide, but his mother, Enju, comes to his aid by arranging for him and Chidori to escape from the mansion. The role of the villainous Heiji is performed in comic fashion and considerably enhances the interest of this act.

Act 3, scene 1, "The Inn at Ōtsu"

In the recent battle at Uji, Kiso Yoshinaka was defeated and killed, and his wife, Lady Yamabuki, with her son Komawaka and their maid Ofude, take shelter for the night at an inn. Sharing the neighboring room are a boatman, Gonshirō, his daughter Oyoshi, and her small son Senmatsu.

Searching for Yamabuki and her son, Genji troops enter the inn. During the resulting confusion, Yamabuki runs from the building with Senmatsu, whom she mistakes in the darkness for her own child. Meanwhile Gonshirō and Oyoshi escape with Komawaka, believing him to be Senmatsu.

Act 3, scene 2, "The Bamboo Stretcher"

Lady Yamabuki and Senmatsu flee to a nearby bamboo grove, where Ofude tries to fight off the Genji troops. Believing him to be Komawaka, a soldier captures the boy and kills him. The shock of this is too much for Yamabuki, who expires. But when the maid Ofude examines the body of the dead child, she realizes the mistake. Ofude then cuts down some bamboo trees to make a stretcher upon which to carry the body of her mistress.

Act 3, scene 3, "The House of Matsuemon"

Gonshirō has been raising Komawaka as his own grandson until the day that the real Senmatsu returns. The maid Ofude, who

42. *Hiragana Seisuiki*, act 3, scene 4, "The *Sakaro* Pine." Higuchi no Jirō fights off the enemy sailors who attack him. During this famous scene, the actors arrange themselves in the shape of a boat with Higuchi in the center.

has been searching for Komawaka, arrives to claim the child. On hearing that Senmatsu is dead, Gonshirō and Ofude vent their anger and grief, and the old man is moved to kill Komawaka. He is stopped, however, by his son-in-law, Matsuemon, who reveals himself to be Higuchi no Jirō Kanemitsu, loyal retainer of Komawaka's dead father, Kiso Yoshinaka. Boatmen then arrive to receive instruction from Matsuemon in the art of "reverse oars" (*sakaro*), a rowing technique that increases a boat's maneuverability in battle.

In the short scene that follows, child actors are used to create a sense of distance as Matsuemon, instructing the sailors, is seen in a boat in the offing. The sailors, however, turn out to be Genji warriors in disguise, come to capture Matsuemon, whom they know to be Higuchi no Jirō.

Act 3, scene 4, "The Sakaro Pine"
The fight continues on land with Matsuemon-Higuchi single-handedly taking on attacking Genji sailors. Surveying the 71

countryside from a small hill, upon which stands a solitary pine tree, Higuchi finds himself surrounded (fig. 42). Hatakeyama Shigetada, a Genji general, arrives with his men and promises to protect the child Komawaka. The safety of the boy assured, Higuchi surrenders and allows himself to be bound. The choreography for the battle in this scene is famous.

Act 4, "The Kanzaki House of Assignation"

Genta is now penniless and is being supported by Chidori, his betrothed, who has become a courtesan with the name of Umegae. Hearing that a battle against the Heike is imminent, Genta is anxious to participate and restore his good name, but he lacks the money to redeem his armor from pawn. Frustrated at being unable to help, Chidori strikes with a ladle the stone basin by the verandah. As she does so, she wishes the basin were the legendary bell of the Kannon Temple so that she might have her wish fulfilled and gain the necessary money. Amazingly, the money materializes (fig. 43), provided from her hiding place by Genta's mother, Enju, who is sympathetic to their plight.

43. *Hiragana Seisuiki*, act 4, "The Kanzaki House of Assignation." The money that Chidori has been wishing for suddenly materializes. To create the effect of a fountain of coins gushing into view, the coins are dangled on the ends of wires which are attached to rods manipulated by a hooded stage assistant.

Ichinotani Futaba Gunki (Chronicle of the Battle of Ichinotani)

This historical drama of 1751 is probably the last involving the playwright Namiki Sōsuke, who is said to have died after completing act 3. Originally in five acts, those still performed today are acts 2 and 3.

Act 2, scene 1, "Before the Heike Camp"

Anxious to be the first to engage the enemy at the battle of Ichinotani, Kojirō (son of the Genji general Kumagai) rushes to the gate of the Heike camp but stands entranced when he hears the sound of a flute coming from inside. Kojirō is followed by Hirayama, who hates him and his father and encourages the boy to storm into the camp.

Kumagai himself then appears and, entering the camp, emerges again with his wounded son. The Heike prince Taira no Atsumori then sallies forth to pursue Hirayama and engage him in combat.

Act 2, scene 2, "Suma Beach"

Some distance away, the fiancée of Atsumori, Princess Tamaori, comes in search of him. Hirayama, who has escaped from Atsumori, notices the girl and makes advances to her. When Tamaori rejects him, Hirayama kills her.

Act 2, scene 3, "Another Part of the Beach"

A "drop curtain" (*asagimaku*) is then used to reveal the next scene, in which Atsumori is killed by Kumagai. Both are on horseback as Kumagai, waving his battle fan decorated with the rising sun, rides into the waves after Atsumori, calling for him to stop and fight. At this point, child actors are substituted to create a sense of distance as, still on horseback, the two make toward each other in the offing. As they fight, they sink under the waves, and shortly afterward the original actors in the roles are seen on the shore, having risen into view on a trap lift.

Kumagai is the victor, but because of Atsumori's extreme youth, decides to allow him to escape. Hirayama notices them, however, so Kumagai has no choice but to decapitate the boy (fig. 6).

73

Act 3, "Kumagai's Camp"

It transpires, however, that it was not Atsumori but his own son, Kojirō, that Kumagai had killed. Before the battle began, Yoshitsune, the leader of the Genji forces, had ordered that Atsumori, as a prince of the blood, was not to be harmed despite his allegiance to the Heike side. The order to this effect, which has been written on a signboard in the form of a cryptic message, also suggests that, if necessary, Kojirō must be sacrificed to protect Atsumori. This alteration of the circumstances of the plot, done without informing the audience, considerably enhances the interest of the latter half of the play.

Concerned for the safety of Kojirō, Kumagai's wife, Sagami, has come to the camp. Fuji-no-kata, the mother of Atsumori, also arrives, having heard that Kumagai has killed her son. When Kumagai himself returns, Fuji-no-kata attacks him with a dagger but is easily disarmed. In a famous recitation, involving much use of his battle fan, Kumagai then describes how he captured and was then forced to kill "Atsumori." One of the most im-

44. *Ichinotani Futaba Gunki*, act 3, "Kumagai's Camp." Grasping the signpost on which is written Yoshitsune's message, Kumagai glares down in a powerful *mie* pose.

portant moments in the play is when Kumagai removes the lid of the box containing the severed head of Kojirō, and Sagami and Fuji-no-kata both rush forward to look. Seizing the wooden post bearing Yoshitsune's message, Kumagai forces the women back and glares down at them in a powerful *mie* pose (fig. 44).

Yoshitsune is satisfied that Kumagai has faithfully carried out his order. But Kajiwara, who has overheard everything, attempts to run off to report to Yoritomo that the head is not that of Atsumori. He is killed, however, by Midaroku, an aged stonemason, who throws a chisel. As Midaroku is about to leave along the *hanamichi*, he is called back by Yoshitsune, who has recognized him as his ancient benefactor. Returning to the main stage, Midaroku reveals his true identity as the warrior Munekiyo. Out of gratitude for Munekiyo's help in the past, Yoshitsune presents him with a box for containing armor, inside which Atsumori is hiding.

Bidding farewell to Yoshitsune, Kumagai removes his helmet and armor to reveal the robes and shaven head of a priest. Proceeding to the *hanamichi*, he rubs his bald pate and laments the impermanence and uncertainty of life in a famous speech that compares his son's short life of sixteen years to the brevity of a dream.

The curtain on the main stage is pulled across, and Kumagai is left alone on the *hanamichi*. The sounds of battle are heard, and Kumagai springs to his feet in readiness to fight. But remembering that he is no longer a warrior but a priest, he makes a hurried exit, hiding his face beneath a straw hat.

Imoseyama Onna Teikin (Exemplary Tales for Women)

This "historical" (*jidaimono*) play was written for the puppet theater by Chikamatsu Hanji, Namiki Shōraku, and others, and first performed in 1771. It was adapted for Kabuki in the same year. Originally in five acts, today only act 3, scene 3, and act 4, scene 4, are normally performed. Occasionally, however, act 4, scene 2 ("The Sugiya Sake Shop") and scene 3 ("The Lovers' Journey"), may be presented. Rich in fantasy and romance, *Imo-* 75 *seyama Onna Teikin* is loosely based on events that took place in the seventh century, particularly the power struggles between the Soga and Fujiwara families to control the fortunes of the imperial line.

Act 3, scene 3, "The Mountains"

Soga no Iruka has seized political power and the emperor has gone into hiding. Anxious to consolidate his position, Iruka issues orders to two high-ranking (but mutually antagonistic) families known for their loyalty to the emperor, that of Daihanji Kiyosumi and the late Dazai no Shōni. Iruka demands that Daihanji's son, Koganosuke, become his retainer and Dazai's daughter, Hinadori, his concubine.

Two *hanamichi* are used for the simultaneous entrances of Daihanji and Sadaka (the widow of Dazai; fig. 20), who each enter with a spray of cherry blossoms, which they are expected to throw into the river Yoshino as a signal to Iruka that their children have agreed to his demands. Oppressed at the thought, the two slowly make their way to their respective mansions on opposite sides of Yoshino River, one at the foot of Mt. Imo, the other of Mt. Se.

45. *Imoseyama Onna Teikin*, act 3, scene 3, "The Mountains." Daihanji uses a bow to guide toward him the head of Hinadori, which, together with items from Hinadori's Doll's Festival set, has been set afloat on the river by Sadaka on the other side.

Unwilling to comply with Iruka's demands, Koganosuke chooses to commit ritual suicide and Hinadori to be decapitated by her mother. To symbolize the posthumous wedding of the two lovers, Sadaka floats the head of Hinadori across the river to the waiting Daihanji on the other side (fig. 45). It is in this way, through the deaths of their children, that two rival families are reconciled.

In a scene of great beauty, the overall effect is greatly enhanced by a magnificent set. Another important point is that the actors in the roles of Sadaka and Daihanji should be of equal experience and skill.

46. *Imoseyama Onna Teikin*, act 4, scene 4, "The Palace." Fukashichi avoids the spears that are thrust up at him through the floor.

Act 4, scene 4, "The Palace"

Because of the temporary ascendancy of Iruka, Fujiwara no Kamatari, who is his chief opponent, has gone into hiding. Kamatari's son, Prince Tankai, has disguised himself and settled in a village near Iruka's palace. There Omiwa, daughter of the proprietor of a sake store, falls in love with him, unaware that he is already engaged to Princess Tachibana, Iruka's younger sister.

In this scene, Iruka is revealed in all his glory surrounded by obsequious courtiers. Possessed of supernatural powers, he is protected by a magic spell that can only be broken by the sound of a flute through which been has poured the blood of a black-hoofed deer mixed with that of a jealous woman.

Kamatari's retainer, Kanawa no Gorō, disguises himself as Fukashichi, a fisherman, and arrives at Iruka's palace with a bottle of sake dangling from the hilt of his sword. He bears a message of congratulation from Kamatari to Iruka and presents the sake as a gift. But the suspicious Iruka declines the sake, which Fukashichi promptly drinks to prove it is not poisoned. Left alone, Fukashichi easily avoids the spears that are thrust at him through the floor (fig. 46), and the poisoned sake he is served he pours onto some flowers, which then shrivel and die. As he is placed under arrest and escorted to another room, Fukashichi casually swings the ends of his long trousers over his shoulder and swaggers off.

Performed in "rough" *aragoto* style, the role of Fukashichi is famous for its humor and a number of important *mie* poses. His fisherman's costume is distinctive. Indeed, he cuts an altogether outlandish figure as he saunters along the *hanamichi* in a padded kimono of broad black-and-white stripes over which he wears formal samurai dress consisting of a winged upper garment and long trailing trousers.

Fukashichi having withdrawn, Omiwa enters in pursuit of her beloved, Prince Tankai, who has preceded her to the palace. There follows one of Kabuki's most pitiful scenes as Omiwa is bullied and humiliated by a group of ugly ladies-in-waiting. She is finally forced to sing a horse-coper's song while dancing at

47. *Imoseyama Onna Teikin*, act 4, scene 4, "The Palace." Omiwa performs the horse-coper's song. In her hand she holds a spool of thread, the end of which was originally attached to the kimono of her beloved.

the same time (fig. 47). After knocking her unconscious, the ladies-in-waiting withdraw, leaving Omiwa alone.

Reviving, Omiwa makes to leave when she hears the ladies-in-waiting congratulating Tankai on his wedding. Believing that the wedding is actually taking place, Omiwa is consumed with jealousy. Her hair falling about her shoulders, she rushes back toward the palace, intending to force her way in. But Fukashichi stops Omiwa and stabs her with his sword. Removing his outer costume, Fukashichi reveals himself as Kanawa no Gorō and explains to the dying Omiwa that, having previously obtained the blood of a black-hoofed doe, it is hers that he now needs— that of a woman killed at the height of a jealous rage. Bidding Omiwa to rejoice for the part she has played in the downfall of Iruka, Gorō thrusts the flute into the wound.

Ise Ondo Koi no Netaba (Mass Murder at Ise)

Written by Chikamatsu Tokusō, *Ise Ondo* was first performed in 1796. Frequently staged, it is a good example of an *engiri* ("severing of relationships") play within the "contemporary" (*sewamono*) genre.

79

A "severing of relationships" usually involves a woman who, believing it the only way to help her lover, pretends that she intends to break with him because she prefers another. Angry and humiliated, the rejected lover later returns to kill the woman, not realizing that her feelings for him are unchanged and that her paradoxical behavior is only a desperate means to help him.

This type of drama was based on a current event and was written and staged at great speed. So, unless the dramatist was competent, this was either impossible or, if the play were finished in time, it would be nothing more than imitation of existing works in a similar vein.

Originally staged for its sensational value, *Ise Ondo* is said to be a dramatization, completed in three days, of an actual incident that occurred in Ise when one man killed nine people. The play is unusual for its setting, the Ise region, and for its skillful depiction of the life of a Shinto priest and that of a courtesan from the licensed quarter. The original play is in four acts, but today only act 3, from the severance scene to that of the murder, is usually performed.

48. *Ise Ondo Koi no Netaba*, act 3, "The Aburaya Teahouse." Manno (left) taunts Mitsugi, who has just suffered the humiliation of being publicly renounced by his lover, Okon (right).

Act 3, "The Aburaya Teahouse"

It is high summer, and in a large room in a teahouse courtesans are seen dressed in light cotton kimonos, fanning themselves in the heat.

Mitsugi, a Shinto priest, is searching for the certificate of authenticity of a certain precious sword. The certificate is in the hands of his enemy, Iwaji. In order to help Mitsugi, his lover Okon goes through the formality of breaking with him (fig. 48) and then entering into an official relationship with Iwaji. The role that heightens this scene, however, is that of the teahouse maid, Manno, who ridicules and torments Mitsugi, leading to bitter antagonism between the two. In addition, the comic role of the low-class courtesan Oshika adds an element of humor and pathos that is not to be found in any other "relation-severing" scene. Another feature is the role of Mitsugi, the Shinto priest, in which strength of character barely disguises a sensual softness in an acting style that combines both "historical" (*jidaimono*) and "contemporary" (*sewamono*) elements.

Oshika is bribed to accuse Mitsugi of having borrowed money from her, and Manno joins in by insulting him, striking him with her fan, and blowing smoke into his face. Though enraged, Mitsugi is caught in a trap and cannot escape. The climax of the scene is when Okon publicly breaks off her relationship with him. Mitsugi is thrown out but soon returns, thinking that he has taken the wrong sword. He then hits Manno with the sheathed weapon, but the scabbard breaks and she is killed. Mitsugi's light summer kimono, mainly of white linen dotted with black spots, becomes stained with blood during the course of this scene, producing a vivid visual effect typical of Kabuki.

Kagami Jishi (New Year's Lion Dance)

A dance to *nagauta* accompaniment, *Kagami Jishi* was first performed in 1893 by Ichikawa Danjūrō IX.

Yayoi, a young lady-in-waiting in Edo Castle, is interrupted in her practice of the tea ceremony and ordered, as part of the New Year celebrations, to perform a felicitous dance involving 81

49. *Kagami Jishi*. The lion as it is teased into a frenzy by butterflies, one of which is visible behind.

the use of a small lion mask held in one hand. As she does so, butterflies fly around her, and the mask, coming alive in her hand, begins to snap at them. The first half of the dance ends with the butterflies disappearing along the *hanamichi*, followed by Yayoi, who is dragged along by the mask, powerless to resist. During an interlude that follows, the spirits of the butterflies reappear in the form of two little girls who perform a short dance.

Meanwhile, Yayoi has been completely possessed by the spirit of the lion and reappears as the animal itself, prancing energetically. Having fallen asleep among sprays of peonies, the lion is awoken by the butterflies, who tease it into a frenzy (fig. 49), causing it to whirl its great white mane around and around.

Lion dances have long existed in the Kabuki repertoire. Belonging to a category of dances known as "Stone Bridge," they derive from the Noh play *Shakkyō*, in which figures a narrow stone bridge spanning a bottomless ravine. On the other side is seen a lion, the guardian of the Bodhisattva of Wisdom.

Kagami Jishi was inspired by the dance *Makura Jishi* (Pillow Lion), in which a courtesan is transformed into a lion. To make the dance more refined and sophisticated according to the tastes of the late nineteenth century, Ichikawa Danjūrō IX changed the courtesan into a lady-in-waiting at the castle of the shogun.

Kanadehon Chūshingura (The Treasury of Loyal Retainers)

Written for the Bunraku by the three great playwrights Takeda Izumo II, Miyoshi Shōraku, and Namiki Senryū, this eleven-act "historical" (*jidaimono*) play was first staged in 1748. The play is based upon events that occurred in the years 1701 and 1702, when Asano Naganori, lord of the provincial fief of Akō, was put in charge of the reception at the shogun's castle in Edo of imperial envoys from the court in Kyoto. Unfamiliar with the protocol, Asano sought instruction from Kira Kōzukenosuke, master of court ceremonial, but failed to provide the customary bribe. Offended, Kira insulted and humiliated Asano, who responded by drawing his sword and wounding him slightly. Asano was ordered to commit ritual suicide the same day, and his lands and property were confiscated. A group of Asano's retainers vowed to take revenge, however, and they did so eighteen months later when they attacked Kira in his mansion and killed him.

This incident created a profound impression on Edo-period society. Only two weeks after the incident had taken place, references to it are believed to have been worked into a play, ostensibly about the Soga brothers, which was performed at the Nakamura-za theater in Edo. Though quickly banned by the authorities, it was followed by many other vendetta plays—including an important one by the great playwright Chikamatsu Monzaemon—all bearing a suspicious resemblance to the Akō incident.

Staged forty-seven years after the original incident, *Kanadehon Chūshingura* is remarkable for its realism, unlike other major Kabuki plays derived from Bunraku, in which the element of fantasy is very pronounced.

In a strategy typical of Kabuki dramatists who wanted to escape government censorship, *Kanadehon Chūshingura* is set in the Ashikaga period (1336–1573) and the location changed from Edo to Kamakura. No other play compares with it for the frequency with which it is performed in its entirety, including the first act, which is unusual for this type of play. The popularity

50. *Kanadehon Chūshingura*, act 1, "The Shrine of Hachiman, the God of War, in Kamakura." Enya Hangan (center) restrains Wakanosuke, who is indignant at the insults of Moronō.

of *Kanadehon Chūshingura* is such that it has always been regarded as a certain remedy for poor houses.

Act 1, "The Shrine of Hachiman, the God of War, in Kamakura"

This act is unique for the puppet that introduces the cast and for the ceremony with which the curtain is opened.

Ashikaga Takauji, the first Ashikaga shogun, has recently defeated his enemy, Nitta Yoshisada. In a ceremony carried out under the supervision of the shogun's younger brother, Tadayoshi, Nitta Yoshisada's helmet is to be presented to the shrine. Various dignitaries are present. They include the malevolent governor of the region, Kōno Moronō, who supervises the ceremony, and his two assistants, the young warlords Enya Hangan and Momonoi Wakasanosuke.

Yoshisada's helmet had previously been given to him by the emperor in a ceremony attended by Kaoyo, wife of Enya Hangan. Never having seen the helmet, which has been picked up from the battlefield with forty-six others, Tadayoshi orders Kaoyo to identify it. When she has done so, Tadayoshi and the others withdraw with the helmet into the shrine, leaving Kaoyo alone with Governor Moronō. Moronō gives her a love letter and attempts to embrace her, but he is interrupted by Wakasanosuke, whom he insults. Furious, Wakasanosuke is about to draw

84

his sword (fig. 50), but refrains from doing so because of the departure of Tadayoshi from the shrine.

Act 2, "The Mansion of Wakasanosuke"

Still angry, Wakasanosuke reveals to his chief retainer, Kakogawa Honzō, his plan to kill Moronō. Honzō gives his silent support by cutting a branch from a potted pine, indicating that Wakasanosuke should, indeed, eliminate Moronō. But no sooner has Wakasanosuke left the room than Honzō rushes on horseback to speak to Moronō.

Act 3, scene 1, "Outside the Gate of the Ashikaga Mansion"

If he kills Moronō, Wakasanosuke will be required to commit ritual suicide, his land and property will be confiscated, and his line and lineage wiped out. To prevent this happening, Honzō attempts to bribe Moronō, who has just arrived in a palanquin, by offering him expensive gifts. Moronō, who is assumed to be inside the palanquin, does not appear. The whole transaction is carried out by Moronō's foolish retainer, Sagisaka Bannai, whose behavior provides much comic relief.

Act 3, scene 2, "The Pine Room"

Wakasanosuke arrives intent on killing Moronō, but Honzō's bribe has worked. Moronō grovels apologetically before Wakasanosuke, who is so disconcerted that he cannot draw his sword and leaves the room in disgust.

51. *Kanadehon Chūshingura*, act 3, scene 2, "The Pine Room." Provoked beyond endurance, Enya Hangan (left) has just struck Moronō on the forehead with his short sword.

Enya Hangan then arrives, and Moronō rebukes him for being late. A letter is then delivered from Hangan's wife, Kaoyo, to Moronō, her reply to his entreaties to become his lover. Reading it and realizing that his advances have been rejected, Moronō proceeds to vent his disappointment and anger on Hangan in a barrage of insults. Goaded beyond endurance, Hangan draws his sword and attacks and wounds Moronō (fig. 51). He is stopped from inflicting further injury by Honzō, who emerges from his place of hiding behind a screen.

Act 3, scene 3, "Before the Main Gate of the Mansion"

Hayano Kampei, Hangan's retainer, accompanied his master to the mansion, but has slipped out to meet his lover, Okaru, a maid-in-waiting in Hangan's household. Hearing the commotion inside the mansion, Kampei attempts to rush inside to his master's assistance but is too late. Full of remorse, he is about to kill himself when Okaru persuades him to come with her to the home of her parents near Kyoto. (This is the original version. Nowadays, however, the dance "Journey of the Bridegroom" is performed in its place, usually after act 4. Dating from 1838, it is a dance showing Okaru and Kampei on their journey from Kamakura to Kyoto. Bannai [Moronō's foolish retainer] and his men overtake and attempt to arrest them, but are easily routed by Kampei. A colorful dance that combines pathos and comedy, it provides some light relief after the preceding tragedy.)

Act 4, scene 1, "The Mansion of Enya Hangan"

Envoys from the shogun bring Enya Hangan the order to commit ritual suicide. Hangan is ready to do so but is waiting impatiently for the arrival of his chief retainer, Ōboshi Yuranosuke. Unable to delay any longer, Hangan stabs himself, at which moment Yuranosuke rushes in along the *hanamichi*. One of the most famous moments of the play, it can be performed in a variety of ways according to various acting and oral traditions. Before he expires, Hangan manages to convey his wish to Yuranosuke that his death be avenged (fig. 52).

Hangan's body is borne away to a temple while the remaining retainers argue among themselves about what to do next.

52. *Kanadehon Chūshingura*, act 4, scene 1, "The Mansion of Enya Hangan." Having removed the suicide dagger, Yuranosuke returns the hand of the dead Hangan to its former position.

The aged Ono Kudayū and his son, Sadakurō, are anxious to lay hands on Hangan's gold. Others wish to resist the order to hand over the mansion to the shogun's men. When Kudayū has left, Yuranosuke persuades the others to vacate the mansion peaceably and to join him later in a vendetta.

Act 4, scene 2, "The Rear Gate of the Mansion"
The stage revolves to show the rear gate of the mansion. The building having been evacuated, Yuranosuke is left alone to make a sad departure from his beloved home. The desolation he feels is enhanced by the sound of the cawing of a crow. The set of the mansion, mounted on wheels, is pulled to the back of the stage, creating an illusion of distance as Yuranosuke makes a slow exit along the *hanamichi*. Written without romantic embellishment, the section of the play from Hangan's suicide to the vacation of the mansion is unusual for its realism.

Act 5, scene 1, "The Yamazaki Highroad"
Hangan's erstwhile retainer Kampei has become a hunter and is living with Okaru and her parents outside Kyoto. As he is out hunting for boar one night, the fuse of Kampei's musket goes out. He asks for a light from a passerby, who turns out to be Senzaki Yagorō, a fellow retainer of Enya Hangan's and a member of Yuranosuke's vendetta group. Kampei expresses his desire to join them and redeem his honor.

Act 5, scene 2, "The Two Musket Shots"
Okaru's father, Yoichibei, has been to Kyoto to arrange the sale of his daughter to a brothel for the sum of one hundred gold

pieces, which money he will give to Kampei to donate to the vendetta group. Returning home with half the money (the rest will be paid when Okaru is handed over to the brothel keeper), he is killed and robbed by Sadakurō, the delinquent son of Ono Kudayū (see act 4, scene 1). As he is about to leave, Sadakurō is accidentally shot dead by Kampei, who mistakes him in the dark for a boar. Examining the body, Kampei discovers the stolen money—though he is unaware of its source—and succumbs to the temptation to steal it himself to donate to the vendetta group.

Although this scene is only incidental to the plot, it is full of interest for its many Kabukiesque features, including Sadakurō's stunning black costume, which powerfully enhances his ominous presence. A brilliant innovation by the actor Nakamura Nakazō (1736–90), it was he who transformed the minor character Sadakurō, who previously had always appeared in the nondescript costume of a mountain brigand, into a major role performed only by leading actors skilled in the portrayal of handsome young men. The stratagem whereby the audience is aware of something that characters in the play are not (in this case, the real circumstances relating to the death of Sadakurō) was also new at the time.

Act 6, "The Suicide of Kampei"

In what is one of the most important acts of the play, Osai, the mistress of the brothel to which Okaru has been sold, arrives with a manservant to collect the girl. The remaining fifty gold pieces are paid to Okaru's mother (Okaya) and the girl is bundled into a palanquin to be carried off when Kampei returns and forces the bearers back to the house.

At first Kampei opposes the sale of Okaru to the brothel. But when he notices that the bag containing the money paid by Osai is identical to that which he stole earlier from the corpse, he concludes that he must have killed Yoichibei, his father-in-law. Bidding her a sorrowful farewell, Kampei allows Okaru to be taken away.

Yoichibei's body is later brought in and Okaya, who has
become increasingly suspicious of Kampei, accuses him of hav-

53. *Kanadehon Chūshingura*, act 6, "The Suicide of Kampei." The explanation of the dying Kampei convinces Hara Gōemon (right) and Senzaki Yagorō that his name should be added to the list of the vendetta group.

ing murdered the old man. Senzaki Yagorō arrives with Hara Gōemon, a senior member of the vendetta group, to tell Kampei that his request to join them has been turned down. Believing Okaya's accusations, they berate Kampei as the murderer of his own father-in-law. In despair, Kampei decides to commit ritual suicide and stabs himself in the stomach. As he is dying, Kampei explains the circumstances of the shooting incident. Senzaki examines the body of Yoichibei and, seeing sword rather than bullet wounds, realizes that the old man was killed by Sadakurō, who was then shot by Kampei. Praising Kampei as Yoichibei's avenger, they add his name to the list of the vendetta group, sealed in his own blood. Kampei is able to die happy (fig. 53).

A tragedy that results from the laudable wish to contribute money to the vendetta group, this act is performed in the "contemporary" (*sewamono*) style.

54. *Kanadehon Chūshingura*, act 7, "The Ichiriki Teahouse in Kyoto." While Yuranosuke peruses the letter by the light of the lantern, Okaru also reads it, with the aid of a mirror, as does Kudayū (just visible) from his position under the verandah.

Act 7, "The Ichiriki Teahouse in Kyoto"

In sharp contrast to the preceding act, Yuranosuke is now seen at his revels in the licensed quarter of Kyoto as he tries to convince his enemies that he has given up his plan of revenge and abandoned himself to debauchery. His son, Rikiya, brings him a letter from the widow of Enya Hangan concerning the movements of Moronō. In one of the most famous moments of the play, Yuranosuke reads the letter by the light of a lantern, unrolling it at the same time so that one end hangs down over the verandah. This gives Ono Kudayū, who is spying on Yuranosuke from beneath the verandah, the opportunity of reading as it slowly comes into view. At the same time, Okaru, who is engaged there as a courtesan, also reads the letter from a window above with the aid of a mirror (fig. 54).

Realizing what has happened, Yuranosuke announces to Okaru that he will buy her contract and release her from the brothel. The delighted Okaru tells her brother, Hei'emon, who has also arrived. Hei'emon realizes, however, that Yuranosuke has only done this so that he can later kill Okaru to guarantee that she leaks no information about the letter. Since she is going to die anyway, Hei'emon asks Okaru to let him kill her so that he can demonstrate his loyalty to his late master, Enya Hangan, and be allowed to join the vendetta group. Yuranosuke, who has overheard this, allows him to join anyway and praises them both for their exemplary conduct. Yuranosuke then helps Okaru to kill Kudayū, still under the verandah, on behalf of her late husband, Kampei.

Act 8, "The Journey of the Bride"

Honzō's daughter, Konami, is betrothed to Rikiya, the son of Yuranosuke. Having heard no more of the matter since the death of Enya Hangan, Honzō and his wife, Tonase, are still anxious for the wedding to take place. In this act, which is performed as a dance, Tonase is seen escorting Konami on the long journey from Kamakura to Yamashina, near Kyoto, where Yuranosuke and his family are now residing. The mood of melancholy is relieved by the arrival of a group of pilgrims on their way to the great shrine at Ise, and also a pair of comic footmen.

Act 9, "The House of Yuranosuke at Yamashina"

Tonase and Konami arrive. But Yuranosuke's wife, Oishi, refuses to agree to the marriage because the death of Enya Hangan was a direct result of the bribe given by Tonase's husband, Honzō, to Moronō. This is too much for Tonase, who decides to kill her daughter and then herself, but when she raises the sword to behead Konami, she is stopped by the sound of a *shakuhachi* flute being played by a mendicant standing at the gate (fig. 7). Tonase's reaction to the sound, and the acting involved, are a great test of the skill of the actor in the part.

The mendicant turns out to be none other than Honzō, who enters and insults Yuranosuke. Rikiya, Yuranosuke's son, attacks Honzō with a spear and wounds him mortally. It turns out, however, that Honzō deliberately provoked the boy into doing so to atone for his part in Hangan's death. Honzō goes on to regret the bribe he offered to Moronō, whose anger was then deflected onto Hangan. By way of further atonement, Honzō produces a map, showing the interior of Moronō's mansion in Edo, which will prove invaluable to Yuranosuke and his men when they make their attack.

Act 10, "The Shop of Amagawaya Gihei"

In an act now rarely performed, Gihei, the proprietor of the Amagawa store, has been entrusted by Yuranosuke with the shipment to Edo of the vendetta group's weapons and equipment. Other members of the group are suspicious of Gihei, however, and posing as policemen, they accuse him of being a party to the vendetta that Yuranosuke is known to be contemplating. Threatening to kill his small son, they order Gihei to open one of the cases containing the weapons, but he refuses. Having put Gihei to the test and not found him wanting, the "policemen" reveal who they are as Yuranosuke himself emerges and apologizes.

Act 11, "The Attack on the Mansion of Moronō"

Yuranosuke and his men launch their attack but are unable to find Moronō. Eventually he is discovered inside a charcoal shed and offered a dagger—the one used by Enya Hangan—with

91

which to kill himself. Moronō takes the dagger but lunges with it at Yuranosuke, who then stabs him.

Having decapitated Moronō, the warriors—forty-seven in all (if the dead Kampei is included)—proceed through the streets to offer the head at the grave of Enya Hangan. On the way, they are stopped by a mounted warrior on guard duty, but when he hears who they are and what they have done, he praises them and allows them to continue.

Kanjinchō (The Subscription Scroll)

Based on the Noh play *Ataka*, *Kanjinchō* (in one act) was written by Namiki Gohei III and first performed in 1840. The last addition to the so-called Kabuki Eighteen (*jūhachiban*), it differs from the others in the use of the lyrical (*nagauta*) ensemble and for the element of dance, which indeed is very strong. The setting is in the *matsubame* style, the conventional Kabuki version of the Noh stage, consisting of a backdrop of a large pine tree that dominates a bare stage.

Minamoto no Yoshitsune, the young hero of the Heike-Genji wars, is fleeing to friendly territory in the north to escape the jealous wrath of his elder half-brother, Yoritomo, the leader of the Genji clan. To stop Yoshitsune, Yoritomo has ordered barriers to be erected at strategic points throughout the country. One of the most important of these barriers is at Ataka, where the action of the play takes place.

Togashi Saemon, who is in charge of the barrier, enters and explains in his speech of introduction the reason for the erection of the barrier: to stop Yoshitsune and his small party of loyal retainers, who are known to be fleeing north disguised as mountain priests (*yamabushi*).

Togashi and his men position themselves at the barrier. A famous passage of lyrical singing (*nagauta*) begins, and Yoshitsune and his party enter along the *hanamichi*. Yoshitsune's men are all for fighting their way past the barrier, but the formidable Musashibō Benkei, Yoshitsune's right-hand man, advises against it. With Yoshitsune bringing up the rear as a porter, Benkei leads the group to the barrier, where he tries to convince Togashi that

55. *Kanjinchō*. Suspicious as to the real identity of the porter, Togashi (right) advances aggressively toward Benkei.

they are on their way to the northern provinces to collect subscriptions toward the rebuilding of the Tōdaiji temple in Nara. Togashi refuses to let them pass. While Yoshitsune sits quietly to the side, his face hidden under a wide straw hat, Benkei and the others perform their last rites as if preparing for death.

Instead of killing them, Togashi surprises Benkei by ordering him to read the subscription scroll (*kanjinchō*), upon which the purpose of the fund raising is explained and people are exhorted to donate generously. Not having such a scroll, Benkei improvises magnificently, pretending to read from one that is blank. As Benkei does so, Togashi tries to catch a glimpse of it. Benkei's pose, as he attempts to keep the scroll from being seen, is perhaps the most famous in Kabuki.

Togashi then interrogates Benkei as to the nature of the beliefs of mountain priests, and the ensuing struggle between the two men is the first important climax to the play. Eventually Togashi gives Benkei permission to pass, but as Yoshitsune is about to go through the barrier he is recognized by one of the guards and ordered to stop (fig. 55). Benkei censures Yoshitsune for causing trouble and, in the second climax, strikes him. Moved by the extent of Benkei's loyalty, which forces him to strike his master in order to save him, the compassionate Togashi—who has long since realized who they are—allows the group to go on its way.

Yoshitsune then thanks Benkei, and this display of gratitude, as well as Benkei's emotional reaction to it, is the third great moment of the play.

Meanwhile, Togashi has followed them with an offer of sake to speed them on their journey. Benkei becomes drunk and performs a "Dance of Longevity." As he does so, he signals to Yoshitsune and the others to make good their escape. The curtain having been drawn on the main stage, Benkei is left alone at the foot of the *hanamichi* to perform his famous "six-direction" (*roppō*) exit, chasing after the others in a series of great leaps and bounds (fig. 18).

Kasane (Disfigured Kasane)

A dance-drama, *Kasane* was first performed in 1823.

Yoemon, a handsome but unscrupulous young warrior absconds from his clan, abandoning his lover, Kasane. The girl catches up with him, however, at the banks of the river Kinu and begs him to join her in a suicide pact. Yoemon seems to agree, but as they make their preparations (fig. 12), a wooden grave marker comes floating downstream bearing a sickle

56. *Kasane*. Yoemon forces Kasane to look into the mirror.

embedded in a skull. Lifting these from the water, Yoemon recognizes the sickle as the one he used to kill the jealous husband of his former lover. Yoemon has never realized that Kasane is the daughter of the man he murdered. Kasane is possessed by her father's vengeful spirit, which makes her limp and disfigures her face. She is unaware of the changes in her appearance, however, and one of the climactic moments of the dance-drama is her reaction when Yoemon forces her to look in a mirror (fig. 56).

Yoemon's evil nature is revealed when, again with the sickle, he strikes at Kasane and wounds her mortally. As he does so, Kasane slips her right shoulder from her sleeve to reveal an under-kimono decorated with autumn leaves. An example of Kabuki aesthetics, the pattern of red leaves is meant to represent blood.

Having killed Kasane, Yoemon attempts to escape, shielding himself from the rain with a straw mat. He is pulled back by Kasane's vengeful spirit.

Kenuki (The Tweezers)

One of the Kabuki "Eighteen" (*jūhachiban*), this "historical" (*jidaimono*) play is, like *Narukami* (Narukami the Priest), an independent piece that was originally part of a longer play staged in 1742 by Ichikawa Danjūrō II. Though long unperformed, *Kenuki* was successfully revived by Ichikawa Sadanji II. It has since become very popular on account of the humor, atmosphere, and exaggerated effects that it retains from the golden age of Kabuki.

"The Mansion of Ono no Harumichi"

Princess Nishiki, daughter of the courtier Ono no Harumichi, is engaged to the young nobleman Bunya no Toyohide. But because of a sudden, strange illness that causes her hair to stand on end, the princess postpones the wedding indefinitely. Suspicious of the circumstances of the "illness," Toyohide sends his retainer Kumedera Danjō to Harumichi's mansion to investigate.

95

As he waits to greet Harumichi, Danjō flirts first with a attractive youth and then a maid who have come to serve him refreshments. On both occasions Danjō makes humorous asides to the audience, apologizing for his scandalous behavior.

In the section of the play to which the title alludes, the bored Danjō produces a large pair of tweezers and begins to pluck hairs from his chin. Inexplicably, the tweezers rise of their own accord and hang suspended in the air (fig. 57).

The farmer Mambei then arrives, who is in league with Gemba, Harumichi's evil chief retainer. Mambei proceeds to accuse Harukaze, Harumichi's son, of having killed his sister, but Danjō realizes that this is part of Gemba's plot to usurp his master's lands and position. Danjō then writes a letter to Emma, the Buddhist guardian of hell, requesting the return of Mambei's sister to the land of the living. Ordering Mambei to deliver the letter in person, Danjō kills him, searches the body, and finds the missing heirloom of the Ono family: a poem in her own hand by Ono no Komachi, the country's greatest woman poet. Taking a spear, Danjō then thrusts it through the ceiling, wounding a hidden spy who falls to the floor clutching a huge magnet.

57. *Kenuki*. The tweezers rise into the air as Danjō wonders what the cause can be.

In this way, Danjō successfully solves the mystery of the princess's illness. The magnet, concealed in the ceiling on Gemba's orders, had made the princess's hair stand on end by attracting her metal hair ornaments. Offering to remove the cause of the unrest in the Ono household, Danjō decapitates Gemba with a single stroke of his sword. Danjō then proceeds to the *hanamichi*, where the actor thanks the audience for their help in the successful performance of a difficult role. For the benefit of the audience, he then executes a powerful *mie* pose and exits nonchalantly along the *hanamichi*.

Koi Bikyaku Yamato Ōrai (Love's Courier on the Yamato Highway)

Written by Chikamatsu Monzaemon in 1711, the present version of this "contemporary" (*sewamono*) play is a later adaptation. There are two acts.

Act 1, "The Izutsuya Teahouse"

Chūbei, the son of a farmer, has been adopted into a family operating a courier service between Osaka and Edo. In love with the courtesan Umegawa, Chūbei intends to ransom her and has already paid some money toward that end. Unfortunately, he is unable to raise the rest and hesitates to go and tell the girl at the teahouse to which she is contracted.

When they do meet, however, Umegawa assures Chūbei of her love for him in spite of his financial problems. But the proprietor of the house warns Chūbei that the money must be raised that very day. Chūbei's rival, the prosperous and belligerent Hachiemon, is also anxious to ransom Umegawa, and there can be no further delay.

Hachiemon arrives with the necessary money and proceeds to malign Chūbei, who listens indignantly from an upstairs room. Pushed beyond endurance, Chūbei rushes in and now claims to have the ransom money. Challenged by Hachiemon to prove it (fig. 58), Chūbei produces several sealed packets of money, which have earlier arrived by courier from Edo and which Chūbei is supposed to be delivering to a customer. Chūbei breaks the seals of the packets, a capital offense, and a stream of golden coins cascades to the floor. Chūbei ransoms Umegawa, to her great joy, but at the same time she is puzzled at the change in Chūbei's behavior and his desperate desire to leave.

58. *Koi Bikyaku Yamato Ōrai*, act 1, "The Izutsuya Teahouse." Hachiemon (center) challenges Chūbei to prove he has the money with which to ransom Umegawa (left).

59. *Koi Bikyaku Yamato Ōrai*, act 2, "Ninokuchi Village." Magoemon, Chūbei's father, slips and breaks the thong of one of his clogs, and Umegawa rushes to his side. The old man recognizes her and yearns to speak to his son.

Act 2, "Ninokuchi Village"

Umegawa now understands the situation and has asked to spend three days with Chūbei as man and wife together before they commit suicide. The remainder of the money spent and the police on their heels, Chūbei takes Umegawa to his native village to pay respects at the grave of his mother.

Recognizing his father, Magoemon, walking home in the snow, Chūbei longs to speak to him but is unwilling to place the old man in the position of having to report his fugitive son to the police. When Magoemon slips and breaks the thong of one of his clogs, the solicitous Umegawa rushes to his side before Chūbei can prevent her. Aware that the old man knows who she is and that he yearns to speak to Chūbei (fig. 59), Umegawa blindfolds him so he can speak to his son without being obliged to report having seen him. The sounds of a pursuit party can be heard, and Magoemon advises them on the best route of escape and urges them to be on their way.

This is another play from the Osaka-Kyoto region in which the element of "soft" (*wagoto*) acting is very strong. The comic aspects of the style are very pronounced in the first act, when Chūbei dithers on the *hanamichi*, unable to decide whether he should meet Umegawa or not. The seal-breaking scene is famous and can be performed in a number of ways, depending on the interpretation of the actor in the role of Chūbei. The climax comes when Chūbei breaks the seals on the packets of money and he alone realizes that he does not have long to live.

Kosode Soga Azami no Ironui (The Tale of Izayoi and Seishin)

Written by Kawatake Mokuami, the "thieves" dramatist, this "contemporary" (*sewamono*) play was first performed in 1859. Of the seven acts, the first and third are the most frequently staged.

Act 1, scene 1, "The Hyapponkui Dike by Inase River"

Because of his love for the courtesan Izayoi, the young priest 99

Seishin is expelled from his temple. Meanwhile Izayoi escapes from the licensed quarter and comes searching for her lover, meeting him accidentally by Inase River. Although Izayoi is pregnant with Seishin's child, they agree that they are unlikely to find happiness in this life and decide to commit suicide (figs. 10, 60). They jump into the river, but Izayoi is saved from drowning by the poet Byakuren, who is fishing from a boat farther downstream.

Seishin—too good a swimmer to drown—emerges with his life from the water, but berates himself for having allowed Izayoi to die alone. He is about to jump into the river once more when a young man, Motome, arrives, who happens to be carrying a large some of money. Anxious to pay for memorial services for Izayoi, Seishin suddenly demands that Motome lend him the money. The young man refuses and a struggle ensues in which he is accidentally killed. Aghast, Seishin prepares to kill himself, but again cannot. He then hears the sound of singing from the nearby licensed quarter, and in a famous speech decides that life is preferable, even the life of crime he now decides upon.

Izayoi and Byakuren appear, but in a scene performed in the "dumb-show" (*dammari*) style, Seishin fails to recognize his lover

60. *Kosode Soga Azami no Ironui*, act 1, scene 1, "The Hyapponkui Dike by Inase River." Izayoi (left) and Seishin have agreed that they are unlikely to find happiness in this world and prepare to commit suicide together.

in the darkness. They go their separate ways, each unaware of the survival of the other.

In the remainder of the play, which is not frequently staged, the two eventually meet again, and Izayoi joins Seishin in his criminal activities. In a denouement typical of the playwright Mokuami, they try to extort money from Byakuren, who turns out to be, not only an arch-criminal, but the brother of Seishin as well.

Kotobuki Soga no Taimen (The Soga Brothers' Confrontation)

Performed annually, like *Shibaraku* (Wait!), this one-act "historical" (*jidaimono*) play was originally one scene from a much longer work that depicted the confrontation between the two brothers, Soga no Gorō and Soga no Jūrō, and their father's killer, Kudō Suketsune. *Soga no Taimen* now exists as an independent piece. The first performance is believed to have taken place circa 1676.

Plays about the Soga brothers were so popular during the Edo period (1603–1867) that, from the Genroku era (1688–1704) onward, they accounted for more than half the repertoire of Edo Kabuki. Initially, the confrontation scene was reworked every year, but the different versions have gradually condensed into the standard form that can be seen today.

The plot involves the warrior Asaina's arranging for the Soga brothers, Jūrō and Gorō, to meet their enemy, Kudō Suketsune, at his mansion. Suketsune gives them free passes to his hunting ground, and the three part for the time being, promising to meet again. Despite the extreme simplicity of the plot, the play is replete with the stylized beauty of classical Kabuki.

The setting is the mansion of Kudō Suketsune. Suketsune is dressed in informal clothes, while Asaina wears long trailing trousers and an outer coat with wide sleeves decorated with a circular crane pattern. Ōiso no Tora and Shōshō, the two lovers of Jūrō and Gorō, are also in attendance, dressed as courtesans. Traditionally, the role of Suketsune is played by the leader of 101

61. *Kotobuki Soga no Taimen.* Gorō (left) is prevented by his brother, Jūrō, from attacking Kudō Suketsune (right), the murderer of their father.

a Kabuki troupe and Tora by the principal female impersonator. Asaina is a clown's role, and those of the guards, Kajiwara and Ōmi, villains. The roles of Jūrō and Gorō represent the romantic lead and the specialist in "rough" (*aragoto*) acting, respectively.

Asaina calls for the two brothers to enter, and Jūrō comes in carrying a New Year's gift. Gorō enters aggressively, stands besides Jūrō, and then starts to go onto the main stage but is gently stopped by Jūrō. This is done to show that Gorō is being performed in the "rough" *aragoto* style and Jūrō in the "soft" *wagoto* style. Asaina's curious way of speaking, involving much use of the nonsense syllables *mosa-mosa*, and his "monkey" makeup are said to have been created by the actor Nakamura Denkurō (1662–1713).

Suketsune offers Gorō a cup of sake served on a wooden stand. The climax to the play occurs when Gorō, unable to control himself in the presence of the his father's murderer (fig. 61), hurls abuse at Suketsune, flings the wine cup to the floor, and crushes the stand.

The play ends with a famous and felicitous pose as Suketsune, standing on a dais, holds his sword and fan in such a way as to represent a crane in flight. Meanwhile, Gorō gestures aggressively toward Suketsune, but is restrained by Jūrō on one side and Asaina on the other. The triangular shape they form 102 is intended to represent Mt. Fuji.

Kuruwa Bunshō (Love Letters from the Licensed Quarter)

In Kabuki of the Kyoto-Osaka region, plays featuring Yūgiri, the courtesan, and her lover, Izaemon, were extremely popular. They also became a vehicle for the actor Sakata Tōjūrō (1647–1709), a master of the "soft" (*wagoto*) style of acting who is known to have performed the role of Izaemon on as many as eighteen different occasions. Chikamatsu Monzaemon later wrote a Bunraku puppet play on the Yūgiri-Izaemon theme which was adapted to Kabuki. *Kuruwa Bunshō* derives from that play and, in a revised form dating from 1808, has become the representative Yūgiri-Izaemon play in the Kabuki repertoire.

Scene 1, "The Yoshidaya Teahouse"

Izaemon, the son of a wealthy Osaka merchant, has squandered a fortune on the courtesan Yūgiri. Penniless and disowned though he is, Izaemon is unable to forget Yūgiri and appears one day at the entrance of the teahouse, dressed shabbily in a paper kimono, his face hidden by a sedge hat. Mistaking him for a beggar, the employees of the house attempt to drive Izaemon away, but he is recognized by the proprietor and invited in to meet Yūgiri, who has been worried sick about him.

62. *Kuruwa Bunshō*, scene 2, "An Inner Room." Izaemon (right) is convinced of Yūgiri's devotion, and there is a tender reunion.

Scene 2, "An Inner Room"

Realizing that Yūgiri is engaged with another customer, the jealous Izaemon frets and sulks as he waits for her. The comic aspect of "soft" (*wagoto*) acting is made clear by Izaemon's antics as he fidgets about the stage, at one point even standing on a table.

When Yūgiri finally appears, Izaemon at first ignores her by feigning sleep. But Yūgiri's delight at seeing him is convincing proof of her devotion, and there is a tender reunion (fig. 62). Meanwhile, Izaemon's mother, deciding to reinstate him, sends a large sum of money, some of which can be used to ransom Yūgiri. The play ends auspiciously with general rejoicing.

Kuruwa Bunshō is highly regarded as the best surviving example of the "courtesan" play, typical of early Kabuki in the Kyoto-Osaka region. The basic elements of such plays (the reunion between an ailing courtesan and her lover, the amiable and cooperative teahouse proprietor, the boxes of gold that arrive to solve everyone's problems) are all fairly faithfully preserved. The play's felicitous theme makes it eminently suitable for performance at the New Year, and this is generally the case.

Meiboku Sendai Hagi (The Disputed Succession)

Written for Kabuki by Nagawa Kamesuke, this "historical" (*jidaimono*) play was first performed in 1777. Of the five acts, the third is rarely performed. The plot is based on a case of disputed succession that shook the important Date fief in 1671.

Act 1, "The Hanamizu Bridge at Kamakura"

Ashikaga Yorikane, an important feudal lord, has been neglecting his duties in favor of disporting himself in the licensed district. As he returns home intoxicated one night, an attempt on his life is made by retainers of Ōe Onitsura, who is eager to usurp Yorikane's position. Yorikane's life is saved by his retainer, the sumo wrestler Tanizō.

Act 2, "The Ashikaga Mansion"

104 Yorikane is to be replaced by his small son, Tsurukiyo. Fearful

for the boy's life, his nurse, Masaoka, keeps a strict watch over him day and night, even scrutinizing the food he eats. In a famous scene Masaoka prepares rice for Tsurukiyo while he plays with Senmatsu, her own son.

In the guise of an official envoy from the shogun, Lady Sakae, wife of one of the leaders in the plot to assassinate Tsurukiyo, arrives with a gift of cakes for the boy. Senmatsu, who is under strict orders from his mother to test Tsurukiyo's food, tastes one of the cakes and declares it to be poisoned. Yashio, an evil lady-in-waiting, is also involved in the plot. She kills Senmatsu, but his mother, the nurse Masaoka, is concerned only for the safety of Tsurukiyo and shows no sign of emotion (fig. 63).

Impressed by Masaoka's composure, Lady Sakae is convinced that the nurse has previously made the two boys change places so that it was Tsurukiyo who was actually killed. Assuming that she can trust Masaoka, Sakae gives her the scroll containing the names of the conspirators.

Sakae withdraws, and in the climax to the scene Masaoka embraces the body of her son and laments his death. Performed only by actors of the highest rank, the role of Masaoka is regarded as one of the most difficult in the repertoire of the female impersonator. Yashio, the evil lady-in-waiting, then returns and tries to kill Masaoka, but it is she who is killed by the nurse. In the confusion, the scroll falls to the floor and is carried off by a large rat.

Act 4, "Under the Floor"

The set is raised to reveal Arajishi Otokonosuke on guard beneath Tsurukiyo's chambers. Performing in "rough" *aragoto* style, Otokonosuke appears on a trap lift, his iron-ribbed fan held above his head and the rat from the previous scene trapped beneath his foot. The rat is, in fact, the arch-villain Nikki Danjō, who is gifted with magic powers. Otokonosuke hits the rat on the forehead, but it escapes down a hole in the *hanamichi*.

Seconds later, Nikki Danjō himself rises into view in a cloud of smoke, the wound still fresh on his brow (fig. 64). Dressed in gray, he makes a famous exit along the *hanamichi* as if walking on air.

105

63. *Meiboku Sendai Hagi*, act 2, "The Ashikaga Mansion." Yashio (right) turns the knife in the throat of the dying Senmatsu, whose mother, Masaoka (left), attempts to hide her feelings as she protects the little lord, Tsurukiyo, who is her charge.

64. *Meiboku Sendai Hagi*, act 4, "Under the Floor." Nikki Danjō (left) rises into view on the *hanamichi* as Otokonosuke looks on.

Act 5, "The Courtroom"

Having failed in his assassination attempt, Ōe Onitsura goes to court to contest the legality of Tsurukiyo's succession to his father's position. The case for Tsurukiyo is argued by his loyal retainer Watanabe Gekizaemon, but the presiding judge, in league with Onitsura and Danjō, finds against Tsurukiyo.

The court is about to rise when a second judge, Hosokawa Katsumoto, arrives. Having been unavoidably delayed, he re-opens the case and, in a brilliant and devastating cross-examination, exposes the plot of Onitsura and Danjō, who are arrested and led away.

Danjō manages to escape, however, and wounds Gekizaemon. The old man tries to flee but is pursued by Danjō, who enters along the *hanamichi* intent on dealing a fatal blow. In a fight scene notable for some magnificent *mie* poses, Gekizaemon attempts to avoid the dagger that Danjō wields, at one point hiding behind a screen on the main stage. Gekizaemon's sons arrive in time to save their father, and Danjō is killed. Katsumoto, the honest judge, enters and congratulates Gekizaemon on the way now being clear for Tsurukiyo to assume his father's position.

Musume Dōjōji (The Maiden at Dōjōji Temple)

One of the greatest Kabuki dances, this was first performed in 1753 by Nakamura Tomijurō I. The plot derives from the famous legend of Kiyohime, a girl who fell in love with a young priest named Anchin who rejected her advances and fled. Furious, Kiyohime pursued him, the extent of her rage causing her to turn into a fire-breathing serpent. The terrified Anchin took refuge at the Dōjōji temple, where he was hidden beneath the temple bell, which was lowered over him. But the serpent only wrapped itself around the bell and melted it, incinerating Anchin in the process.

This legend is celebrated in the Noh play *Dōjōji* (Dōjōji Temple), in which the vengeful spirit of Kiyohime, anxious to destroy the new bell that has recently been installed to replace the one melted by the serpent, arrives in the disguise of a dancing girl.

In the Kabuki version, the curtain opens to reveal the new bell suspended over the stage. The dedication ceremony for the bell is to take place, and the monks enter greatly excited. Hanako, the dancing girl, arrives, and although the presence of women is specifically forbidden, the monks are struck by her beauty and agree to her request to be allowed to dance in honor of the bell.

Wearing a golden hat, Hanako is then revealed inside the grounds of the temple, which is surrounded by mountains covered in cherry blossoms. She then begins her dance, the first part of which is performed with a fan in the slow, stately style of the Noh (fig. 11).

107

65. *Musume Dōjōji*. The dancing girl reveals her true serpent nature as she poses on top of the bell she has caused to crash to the ground.

The mood changes abruptly, however, as a "pull-out" (*hikinuki*) costume change is effected on the stage, in full view of the audience, with the dancer transformed into a young city girl. The dance then proceeds in a series of sections, each involving a change of kimono, some of which require the use of small properties, others being performed without as pure "hand dance." The most difficult section is that in which the dancer describes the emotions of a girl in love. Finally revealing her serpent nature, the girl causes the bell to crash to the ground and poses on it triumphantly (fig. 65).

In another, longer version, the bell falls over the girl, who later emerges, completely transformed into a serpent, and tries to leave by the *hanamichi*. She is stopped, however, by a heroic figure who forces her back to the main stage and there overcomes the serpent in vigorous *aragoto* style. The dance ends with the serpent posing on a red dais while subsidiary actors, wearing identical scale-patterned costumes, arrange themselves as the body and tail. Meanwhile the hero who forestalled the demon's escape performs a dynamic *mie* pose.

Musume Dōjōji is one of the most important dances in the repertoire. Its greatness as a work of art lies in the fact that it is pure Kabuki in concept and entirely free of the Noh original.

108

Narukami (Narukami the Priest)

Also one of the Kabuki "Eighteen" (_jūhachiban_) plays, this "historical" (_jidaimono_) play of one act is now an independent piece that was originally part of a long work which was first staged in 1742.

Because of the grudge he bears the emperor, Narukami, a priest of great virtue and saintliness, has used magic powers to trap the dragon god of rain in a pool at the foot of a waterfall. The result is a drought throughout the land that causes much suffering to the common people. Court officials send the beautiful Princess Taema to seduce Narukami, so that the spell will be broken and rain will fall again. The interest of the play lies in its harmless eroticism and the transformation that Narukami undergoes from saint to devil.

The setting shows Narukami's retreat at the foot of a ravine deep in the mountains. Near at hand are the waterfall and the pool in which the dragon is confined. Princess Taema arrives and asks to become Narukami's disciple. Entranced by the alluring manner in which she introduces herself, Narukami accidentally falls from his position in front of the altar at which he had been praying. Taema then complains of illness, and the distress she affects and the intimate attentions of the priest are delightful.

Persuaded by Taema to drink sake, Narukami becomes intoxicated and leads the girl to his cell (fig. 66). Later, while Narukami sleeps, Taema cuts the sacred rope in front of the

66. _Narukami_. Having drunk sake with Princess Taema, Narukami (left) withdraws with her to his cell.

67. *Narukami*. Narukami awakens in a rage to find that the drought he caused has been brought to an end by Princess Taema's release of the dragon god of rain.

waterfall and the spell is broken. The dragon escapes and rain begins to fall.

Incensed at having been tricked, Narukami changes into a raging demon (fig. 67) and hurls volumes of sacred texts at the acolytes, who try to stop him. Rushing to the foot of the *hanamichi*, he then executes a famous "six-directions" (*roppō*) exit as he sets off in pursuit of Princess Taema (fig. 3).

Natsu Matsuri Naniwa Kagami (Summer Festival in Osaka)

This "contemporary" (*sewamono*) play was written by Namiki Senryū, Miyoshi Shōraku, and Takeda Izumo II, and was first performed in 1745. Originally in nine acts, only acts 3, 6, and 7 are now regularly performed.

Act 3, "In Front of the Sumiyoshi Shrine in Osaka"
Danshichi, a fishmonger, is also a type of townsman known as a "chivalrous commoner"—one who takes it upon himself to protect the interests of the poor against those of the warrior class and who is invariably a member of a gang of like-minded individuals bound by powerful ties of loyalty.

Danshichi is released from prison, where he has served a sentence for wounding a samurai warrior. He is met by the elderly Sabu, also a "chivalrous commoner," who has brought him clean clothes. Danshichi takes them, enters a nearby barbershop for a haircut and shave, and emerges looking a new man.

Kotoura, a courtesan, then enters pursued by Sagaemon, a warrior, who catches up with her and tries to drag her away. Sagaemon, it turns out, is the enemy of Danshichi's own benefactor, Hyōdayū, also a warrior. In fact, it was for wounding one of Sagaemon's men that Danshichi was imprisoned. Danshichi saves Kotoura and beats Sagaemon, who runs off. Meanwhile Kotoura also leaves to be with her lover, Isonojō, the son of Hyōdayū, who is nearby.

Sagaemon then returns with his mercenary, Tokubei, also a "chivalrous commoner." Tokubei and Danshichi fight, but they are stopped by Danshichi's wife, Okaji (fig. 68), who has come with their small son to meet her husband. When it turns out that Tokubei is really loyal to Hyōdayū, he and Danshichi settle their differences and swear eternal friendship.

Act 6, "The House of Sabu"
To protect them from their enemies, Sabu is sheltering Isonojō and Kotoura at his house. Otatsu, the beautiful wife of Tokubei, arrives and, since she is shortly to leave for her home in the coun-

68. *Natsu Matsuri Naniwa Kagami*, act 3, "In Front of the Sumiyoshi Shrine in Osaka." Okaji, the wife of Danshichi (right), brings to a halt the quarrel between her husband and Tokubei.

69. *Natsu Matsuri Naniwa Kagami*, act 7, "A Back Lane in Nagamachi." His body covered in tattoos, Danshichi fights with his father-in-law, Giheiji.

try, agrees to take Isonojō with her, the better to protect him. Sabu, however, feels that Otatsu is too young and beautiful to travel with Isonojō, who has a dissolute reputation. Otatsu takes offense at this insinuation and presses red-hot tongs against her face. Impressed, Sabu agrees to let her travel with Isonojō.

Act 7, "A Back Lane in Nagamachi"

Kotoura is abducted by Giheiji, Danshichi's avaricious father-in-law, who is anxious to make money by selling her. Offering to pay himself for the girl's release, Danshichi persuades Giheiji to let Kotoura be taken back to Sabu's house. But when Giheiji realizes that he has been tricked and that Danshichi does not have the money, the old man becomes angry and insults him. The two begin to struggle and, in a fight scene famous for its formal beauty and *mie* poses (fig. 69), Danshichi first wounds Giheiji and then kills him.

Danshichi, his body covered with mud, then washes himself with buckets of real water from a well. The festival procession that can be heard in the background during the course of the fight then erupts onto the scene, and Danshichi escapes by mingling with the crowd.

Rokkasen (Six Poets)

First staged in 1831, this is one of the most important of the "transformation" (*hengemono*) type of dances. It takes its name from the "Rokkasen," the six great poets of the ninth century: Sōjō Henjō, Ariwara no Narihira, Bunya no Yasuhide, Kisen Hōshi (fig. 70), Ōtomo no Kuronushi, and the one woman in the group, Ono no Komachi. The accompanying music is in the *gidayū*, *kiyomoto*, and *nagauta* styles.

Rokkasen is the only "transformation" piece still likely to be performed in its entirety. It consists of five sections, in each of which one of the male poets pays court to Ono no Komachi, only to be rejected. Originally the roles of the five male poets were meant to be danced by the same actor, but this is never the case nowadays.

In the final section, Ono no Komachi engages the disguised Ōtomo no Kuronushi in a poetry-writing competition and exposes his plot to usurp the emperor's position and seize power. In a sudden transformation Kuronushi reveals who he really is and, standing on a dais and holding a sword over his head, performs a great *mie* pose.

70. *Rokkasen.* Kisen, the priest, dances with Okaji, a waitress from a nearby tea shop, who represents the legendary beauty of the tenth century, Ono no Komachi.

Sagi Musume (The Heron Maiden)

A dance performed to the accompaniment of *nagauta* music, *Sagi Musume* was first staged in 1762.

The setting is the side of a lake on a snowy night in winter. A heron, the reincarnation of a girl who had died rejected by her lover, appears at the water's edge in the shape of a bride in pure white clothes (fig. 71). The effect is that of a figure that has stepped out of a woodblock print, and the accompanying song tells of the uncertainty of love as the dance of the maiden expresses her resentment and jealousy. The whole of this opening sequence is imbued with melancholy but, at the same time, conveys a subtle erotic charm.

The mood changes abruptly as the dancer's outer kimono is removed and the heron is transformed into the spirited city girl it once was. A cheerful atmosphere prevails as she performs a lively dance and plays with a parasol.

Another costume change takes place and the girl is transformed, again, into the heron itself, which beats its wings desperately as it is seen enduring the torments of hell. The dance comes to an end as the heron-maiden poses with a branch of willow leaves.

71. *Sagi Musume*. The heron maiden, dressed in white like a bride, dances at the side of a lake.

Sagi Musume now combines both modern and traditional choreography. At the same time, it preserves, like *Musume Dōjō-ji*, the qualities of Kabuki dance as it was when it was the exclusive domain of the female impersonator.

Sambasō (Felicitous Sambasō)

In the repertoire of the classical Noh drama, the oldest play is *Okina* (literally, "Old Man"). More ritual than entertainment, it is a prayer to the gods for peace and prosperity, consisting of an opening song, a slow dance (performed by the characters Senzai and Okina), and a final fast and lively dance by the character Sambasō.

Okina was adopted into the Kabuki repertoire as *Okina Watashi* (Okina Purifies the Stage), a celebratory dance that, in the Edo period, was performed at the New Year, during the first three days of the new theatrical year (in November), and at the opening ceremony for a newly constructed theater. At such times, the proprietor of the theater would perform the role of Okina, his son that of Senzai, and the principal actor of male roles (or the chief choreographer), Sambasō. In the Noh original, the most important of the three characters is Okina, but in Kabuki, Sambasō attracts most of the attention. The lively and unconventional Sambasō section suited Kabuki in mood and spirit, inspiring the creation of a whole category of Sambasō dances. The most frequently staged in Kabuki are *Shitadashi Sambasō* and *Ayatsuri Sambasō*.

Shitadashi Sambasō (Tongue-Poking Sambasō) was first performed in 1812. The curious title refers to a section of the dance during which Sambasō playfully sticks out his tongue (fig. 72). The first part of the dance sees Senzai and Sambasō dancing together, the latter half Sambasō dancing alone. In addition to his striped hat, Sambasō wears his kimono informally (i.e., without *hakama* trousers), which is unusual.

Ayatsuri Sambasō (Puppet Sambasō) is unusual in that Sambasō dances as if he were a puppet on strings (fig. 73). At the first performance, in 1853, the roles of Senzai and Okina were ap- 115 parently danced in the same way, but now they are performed conventionally.

When Okina and Senzai have concluded their dances and withdrawn, the puppet Sambasō is removed from its box. Its strings having been checked, it is then made to dance about the stage in a delightful and energetic way. The role is a difficult one, not only for the acrobatic element that is introduced when a string breaks or becomes tangled but also for the coordination that is necessary between the dancer and the onstage assistant who plays the puppeteer.

72. *Sambasō*. Sambasō playfully sticks out his tongue.

73. *Ayatsuri Sambasō*. Sambasō's imaginary strings become tangled, and the puppeteer (left) attempts to unravel them.

74. *Sanja Matsuri*. The figures of two fishermen come to life and perform an energetic dance.

Sanja Matsuri (Sanja Festival)

Performed to *kiyomoto* accompaniment, this dance was first staged in 1832.

It is based on the Sanja Festival, one of the biggest in Edo, which celebrated, among other things, the discovery by some fishermen of a statue of Kannon, the Buddhist goddess of mercy, in the river Sumida. The festival also involved a number of wheeled floats upon which were mounted various figures.

One such float shows the figures of two fishermen in a boat. These come to life and perform a dance (fig. 74) which begins with their finding in their net the Kannon statue.

Later a black cloud descends and the fishermen become possessed, one by the spirit of evil, the other by the spirit of good. Each wearing a mask (one marked with the Chinese character ''Good,'' the other with that for ''Evil''), they perform a curious and lively dance, one of the most energetic in the repertory, the balletlike movements of which had never before been seen on the Kabuki stage.

Seki no To (Love at the Osaka Barrier)

A major dance-drama in the repertory, this piece was first performed in 1784. The musical accompaniment is *tokiwazu*.

Seki no To was originally one act from a much longer work, 117

75. *Seki no To*. Kuronushi (right) menaces Sumizome with his axe.

the rest of which has been lost. For that reason, there are a number of obscurities, but that is not a great disadvantage; Kabuki dances do not greatly suffer from gaps in the plot, and in this case the merits of the piece are such that it is regarded as a masterpiece.

The dance, which is divided into two distinct halves, is ostensibly set in the ninth century. The emperor has recently died, and Ōtomo no Kuronushi is planning to usurp the imperial power. He is opposed, however, by two brothers, Munesada and Yasusada, loyal retainers of the late emperor. Also involved are Ono no Komachi and the courtesan Sumizome (both played by the same actor), the respective lovers of the two brothers.

Kuronushi disguises himself as Sekibei, the guardian of a barrier recently erected on Mt. Osaka. Munesada lives nearby, and also in the vicinity is a great cherry tree which, despite it being winter, is mysteriously in bloom, although its blossoms are black.

Ono no Komachi arrives at the barrier. At first, Sekibei refuses to let her pass, but eventually relents so that she can be reunited with her lover. Komachi describes her love for Munesada, and Sekibei dances with them, a section imbued with a relaxed mood typical of works such as this, created during the Temmei period (1781–89). But Sekibei drops the imperial seals that he has previously stolen as part of his plot. Munesada becomes even

118

more suspicious when a hawk brings him the bloodstained sleeve of his brother, who has been attacked and wounded by Sekibei's (i.e., Kuronushi's) men. Sekibei having withdrawn, Ono no Komachi goes to fetch help while Munesada retires to offer prayers for the late emperor.

In the second half of the dance, Sekibei becomes drunk and notices the stars reflected in his great bowl of sake. Performing a powerful *mie* pose, he interprets this as a sign that, if he makes a burnt offering with wood from the cherry tree, his plans to become emperor will be realized. Seizing a huge axe, he attempts to cut down the tree, but he is thwarted by the spirit of the tree, which materializes in the shape of the courtesan Sumizome, lover of the brother Yasusada. The mood changes as Sekibei and Sumizome perform a dance portraying a courtesan and her client in the licensed quarter. Eventually, however, the two reveal their respective true identities by means of the *bukkaeri* costume transformation.

Revealed as a court noble, with a magnificent mane of hair, Kuronushi announces that he plans to control the world. Seizing his axe again, he fights with Sumizome. Kuronushi appears to have the upper hand as, grimacing and sticking out a vivid red tongue, he leans over Sumizome, who poses in a beautiful backbend (fig. 75). Sumizome eventually triumphs, however, and poses on a dais while Kuronushi grips his axe and glares.

Sesshū Gappō ga Tsuji (Gappō and His Daughter)

Originally a Bunraku play, this "historical" (*jidaimono*) piece was written by Suga Sensuke and Wakatake Fuemi and first performed in 1776. Its theme is an unusual one: the love of a stepmother for her stepson. For this reason the play has occasionally been banned. The difficult role of the stepmother, Lady Tamate, is performed only by leading actors. Normally, only act 3 is now staged.

Act 3, "Gappō's Hermitage"
Gappō is a former warrior who now spends his time collecting donations toward the construction of a shrine dedicated to Em- 119

76. *Sesshū Gappō ga Tsuji*, act 3, "Gappō's Hermitage." Tamate comes between Shuntokumaru (right) and his fiancée, Asaka.

ma, the Buddhist guardian of hell. Scandalized by the news of their married daughter's illicit love for her stepson, Gappō and his wife, Otoku, decide that as far as they are concerned she is as good as dead, and hold a memorial service for the repose of her soul. As they do so, Tamate arrives and asks to be let in. The sound of their daughter's voice places the old couple in a quandary. But by reasoning that it is not their daughter but her ghost, they decide to open the door. Tamate, however, has only come on account of her stepson, Shuntokumaru, whom Gappō is sheltering. Although Shuntokumaru is blind and has been disfigured by leprosy, Tamate brazenly declares her passion for him, so mortifying her father that he threatens to kill her. But her mother intervenes and escorts Tamate to another room.

Accompanied by his betrothed, Asaka, Shuntokumaru enters, but hardly has he done so than Tamate returns. Despite his pitiful condition, she makes an impassioned declaration of love, much to his embarrassment. Her hair falling about her shoulders in disarray, Tamate reveals that it was she who caused his blindness and leprosy by giving him poisoned sake to drink. Losing control, she poses threateningly with a knife (fig. 76). Gappō, provoked beyond endurance, takes his sword and stabs her.

As she is dying, Tamate explains how her professed love for
Shuntokumaru, as well as the poison that she gave him, were
intended to drive him away from home so as to save him from
his younger half brother, who was plotting to kill him. She further reveals that Shuntokumaru can be cured by drinking the
blood of a woman born in the year, month, day, and hour of
the tiger. These are the exact circumstances of her own birth,
and it turns out that it was her intention to provoke her father
into killing her so that her blood could be used to restore Shuntokumaru's health and sight. This is what happens, and to the
sound of Gappō's prayer-bell, which he strikes in time to the
sutras he chants, Tamate expires.

Shibaraku (Wait!)

Originally one act from a longer play, this "historical" (*jidaimono*)
play derives its name from the shouts of "Shibaraku" (Wait!)
made from offstage by the hero before he actually appears. It
was first performed in 1692 and was later included in the Kabuki
"Eighteen" (*jūhachiban*). The author's identity is unclear.

During the Edo period, *Shibaraku* was an essential part of the
annual "face-showing" (*kao-mise*) production that took place annually in November. The purpose in doing so was to demonstrate
the pure art of the "rough" (*aragoto*) acting, the hereditary style
of the Ichikawa Danjūrō line of actors, one that involves
something more than mere gratuitous displays of violence upon
the stage. The "rough" style also contains elements of childlike
and innocent humor, and it is these aspects that have made it
increasingly difficult to perform well today.

"The Shrine of the Hachiman, the God of War, at Kamakura"
The evil Kiyohara no Takehira is revealed in all his splendor
flanked by his retainers as well as guards whose bright red bodies
are exposed and their bellies thrust out. Intent on usurping the
position of the emperor, Takehira has captured his principal op-
ponents. He is about to have them put to death when shouts
of "Shibaraku" (Wait!) are heard, filling all assembled with fear. 121

77. *Shibaraku*. The timely intervention of Kamakura no Gongorō (center) saves the lives of the intended victims (lower left) of the evil Takehira (right).

The young warrior Kamakura no Gongorō Kagemasa enters along the *hanamichi* wearing a gigantic sword and a fantastic costume, the outer part of which consists of long trailing trousers and huge persimmon-colored sleeves. His hair is elaborately arranged with paper wings symbolizing power.

Still on the *hanamichi*, Gongorō delivers a famous speech which, as well as being abusive of Takehira, contains obligatory references to the Ichikawa line of actors and its acting traditions. Formerly rewritten every year, this speech has now attained a more or less fixed form.

Takehira's retainers, among whom are a comic priest and a woman, try to persuade Gongorō to withdraw, but he defies them and proceeds onto the main stage. There he poses triumphantly and sets the prisoners free (fig. 77). Foot soldiers attack him, but he decapitates them all with a single stroke of his sword. His mission successfully completed, Gongorō performs a famous ''six-directions'' (*roppō*) exit, roaring the nonsensical words ''yat-toko tottcha untoko na'' as he goes.

More than a play, *Shibaraku* is a time-honored ritual based on the folk tradition of good expelling evil. The semihumorous plot, replete with witty wordplay, reflects the pleasure-seeking spirit typical of the common people in the Edo period.

122

Sugawara Denju Tenarai Kagami (Sugawara's Secrets of Calligraphy)

One of the great Kabuki masterpieces deriving from the Bunraku repertoire, this "historical" (*jidaimono*) play, in five acts, was first performed in 1746.

Sugawara no Michizane (845–903), whose name appears in the title of this work, was a calligrapher, poet, and politician who is now worshiped as the patron saint of learning. In his lifetime he rose to the important position of Minister of the Right at the imperial court, and the play deals with the rivalry between himself and the evil Fujiwara no Shihei, who was Minister of the Left. Other plots include that of three brothers: the triplets Matsuōmaru, Umeōmaru, and Sakuramaru.

The three principal authors of the play (Takeda Izumo II, Namiki Senryū, and Miyoshi Shōraku) are said to have competed against each other in the writing of a scene of parting between a parent and child, and this resulted in act 2, scene 3 ("Dōmyōji Temple"), act 3, scene 2 ("Sata Village"), and act 4, scene 3 ("The Village School"), all of which are based on that theme. "The Village School" is the most famous and the most frequently performed as an independent play.

Act 1, scene 1, "The Imperial Palace"

An ambassador from China arrives at the court anxious to paint a portrait of the emperor, who, however, is ill. Fujiwara no Shihei offers to pose in the emperor's place, wearing the imperial robes. Sugawara no Michizane, knowing of Shihei's plans to usurp the emperor's position, overrules him. (Long unperformed, this act was successfully revived at the National Theater in 1966.)

Act 1, scene 2, "The Banks of the River Kamo"

Prince Tokiyo, the emperor's younger brother, and Kariya, Michizane's adopted daughter, are in love. Sakuramaru, a footman in Tokiyo's service, and his wife arrange for the lovers to enjoy a secret rendezvous in a carriage beside the river Kamo, but the young couple are seen by one of Shihei's spies and forced to go into hiding. This incident helps to explain the rest of the play, but despite this, and regardless of the two charm- 123 ing love scenes—between the royal couple and also between Sakuramaru and his wife—this scene is rarely performed.

Act 1, scene 3, "The Transmission of the Secrets of Calligraphy"
Not only a politician but a master calligrapher as well, Michizane is ordered by the emperor to nominate his successor in the art. While Takabe Genzō, now the principal of a village school, is Michizane's best pupil, he was dismissed from Michizane's service for having fallen in love with Tonami, a maid-in-waiting in the same household. The two have since married and are running a small village school. Despite this, Michizane recalls Genzō and makes him his successor in the art of calligraphy, handing him a scroll containing the ultimate secrets of the art.

Michizane is then summoned to attend on the emperor. Having dressed himself in his best robes, Michizane's hat falls off, and this is interpreted as a bad omen. Later, Shihei accuses Michizane of wanting to put Prince Tokiyo on the throne so that Tokiyo's prospective wife, who is Michizane's daughter Kariya, will become empress. Although he is innocent of these charges, Michizane is ordered into exile. Since Michizane's son and heir, Kan Shūsai, is now also in danger from Shihei, Genzō and his wife escape with the boy and take him to their home in the country.

Act 2, scene 3, "Dōmyōji Temple"
This important scene is reckoned impossible to perform well unless all the leading actors are of similar rank and skill.

The love affair between Michizane's daughter Kariya and the imperial heir is the reason behind Michizane's disgrace and exile. Angry at Kariya for the trouble she has caused, Michizane's elderly aunt, Kakuju, beats her with a stick.

An official escort is expected, at cockcrow, to take Michizane into exile. Kakuju's son-in-law, Sukune no Tarō, and his father, Hyōe, are in league with Shihei, who is anxious to murder Michizane before he goes into exile. Sukune no Tarō and his father cause a cock to crow in the middle of the night and a false escort arrives (in advance of the official one) to take Michizane away. Aware of the plot, Michizane places a wooden statue of himself in the palanquin, which the unsuspecting escort takes

124

away. When the real escort arrives, Michizane is ready to leave with them, but first he bids a sorrowful farewell to his beloved daughter Kariya.

78. *Sugawara Denju Tenarai Kagami*, act 3, scene 1, "The Struggle for the Carriage." Sakuramaru (left) and Umeōmaru (right) stop the carriage containing Lord Shihei and seize a giant parasol. Shihei's retainer—the third brother, Matsuōmaru—intervenes and a stylized confrontation takes place.

79. *Sugawara Denju Tenarai Kagami*, act 3, scene 2, "Sata Village." Sakuramaru (left) commits ritual suicide and Shiratayu chants sutras to the rhythmic accompaniment of the prayer bell he strikes.

Act 3, scene 1, "The Struggle for the Carriage"

In a scene performed in elaborate "rough" (*aragoto*) style, Sakuramaru and Umeōmaru (who are loyal to Michizane) stop the carriage bearing Lord Shihei to a shrine. The third brother, Matsuōmaru, who is in Shihei's service, stops the other two and a violent struggle develops (fig. 78). The music and set for this scene, as well as the costumes, wigs, and *kumadori* makeup, are remarkable. There is also the famous "six-directions" (*roppō*) exit of Umeōmaru and the tug-of-war over the carriage.

The carriage having been broken in the struggle, Shihei himself emerges, making an impressive and malevolent figure in his court dress and eery blue makeup. A typical example of the evil court-noble role, Shihei is normally only performed by leading actors.

Act 3, scene 2, "Sata Village"

Shiratayū is the father of the three brothers and a loyal retainer of Michizane's. To honor the occasion of his seventieth birthday, the three brothers and their wives assemble at Shiratayū's house, but a quarrel develops between Umeōmaru and Matsuōmaru. As they fight with heavy bales of rice, they accidentally break a branch from the cherry tree in the garden, which bodes ill. Sure enough, Sakuramaru commits suicide in order to atone for his part in arranging the meeting between Kariya and Prince Tokiyo (fig. 79). The pathos of this scene is enhanced by the youth of Sakuramaru, the desolated wife that he leaves behind, and his grieving father, whose loyalty to Michizane obliges him to endure and live on.

Act 4, scene 1, "Mt. Tempai"

Angry at the attempt on his life, and also at Shihei's machinations to usurp imperial power, Michizane transforms himself into the god of thunder in order to punish his enemies. Performed in "rough" (*aragoto*) style, this scene is now rarely staged.

Act 4, scene 3, "The Village School"

This, the most famous scene in the whole play, is frequently performed as an independent piece. The scene belongs to the substitution type, an important category in Kabuki.

126

Genzō is hiding Michizane's son, Kan Shūsai, at his village school in the country. On the same day that an unusually gentle child named Kotarō, of refined looks and bearing, is enrolled by his mother at the school, Genzō is ordered to behead Kan Shūsai and present his head for inspection. As Genzō discusses with his wife his plan to behead Kotarō and pass off his head as that of Kan Shūsai, Matsuōmaru arrives, whose duty it is to inspect the head, along with his colleague, Gemba. Since he is meant to be sick, Matsuōmaru wears his hair in the elaborate "hundred days" style and supports himself with his sword, using it as a cane. His magnificent kimono, decorated with snow-covered pine trees, emphasizes the tragic nature of the role.

Matsuōmaru's inspection begins at the gate of the school. In order to make sure that Kan Shūsai is not trying to escape disguised as one of the other children, he examines the face of each child, including that of the school dunce, Yodarekuri, whose antics provide comic contrast to the tragedy that follows.

Ordered to produce the head of Kan Shūsai, Genzō withdraws and returns with that of Kotarō, whom he has just decapitated. Matsuōmaru's reaction to the sound of the decapitation—he staggers and makes an impressive *mie* pose—is one of the great moments of the play. The climax is Matsuōmaru's inspection of the head of Kotarō, which he accepts as that of Kan Shūsai (figs. 5, 80).

When Matsuōmaru and Gemba have left, Genzō attempts to kill Chiyo, the mother of Kotarō, who returns for her son. But

80. *Sugawara Denju Tenarai Kagami*, act 4, scene 3, "The Village School." Matsuōmaru prepares to inspect the decapitated head of his own son.

Chiyo blocks Genzō's sword with Kotarō's school box, from which a child's shroud falls to the floor.

At that moment, Matsuōmaru returns and reveals that Kotarō was his own son, whom he had deliberately enrolled at the school so that he could take the place of Kan Shūsai. Alternately laughing and weeping, Matsuōmaru grieves for his son while rejoicing that the boy has served his purpose, as a substitute for Kan Shūsai, and was not afraid to die.

Removing their outer garments to reveal white mourning dress beneath, Matsuōmaru and Chiyo, as well as Genzō and Tonami, burn incense for the safe journey of their son to the other world. As they do so, the chanter, accompanied by the shamisen player, sings a moving lament for the death of Kotarō.

Act 5, "The Disaster at the Imperial Palace"

Michizane has since died in exile. A series of disasters befalls the court, caused by Michizane in his manifestation as the god of thunder. Eventually Kariya and Kan Shūsai kill Shihei, and calm is restored. The house of Michizane is reinstated, and to placate his angry spirit, Michizane is deified. This act is not often performed but has been successfully revived at the National Theater.

Sukeroku Yukari no Edo Zakura (Sukeroku, Flower of Edo)

This "contemporary" (*sewamono*) play, in one act, is one of the most famous plays in the repertoire and a member of the Kabuki "Eighteen" (*jūhachiban*) group. It was first performed in 1713.

The setting—the scarlet exterior of the Miuraya bordello in the Shin-Yoshiwara district of Edo—is magnificent as the courtesan Agemaki makes her entrance along the *hanamichi*. Sumptuously dressed, she walks on high wooden clogs in what is one of the great visual moments of the play.

Ikyū then enters with his underlings and, having made his way to the main stage, speaks disparagingly of Sukeroku. Agemaki springs energetically to the defense of her favorite and, in a famous speech, compares Sukeroku to the ocean while Ikyū is
128 nothing more than a splash of ink in an inkwell.

81. *Sukeroku Yukari no Edo Zakura*. Courtesans outside the Miuraya bordello look on admiringly as Sukeroku dances, holding a "snake-eye" umbrella.

The success or failure of the play depends upon Sukeroku's entry, which follows. Representing the ideal of the chivalrous commoner, Sukeroku is dressed in the height of fashion—a stylish black kimono and purple headband—and his dance of entry along the *hanamichi*, which involves much posing and posturing with an umbrella, is performed to the accompaniment of music known as *katōbushi*, the only occasion it is heard on the Kabuki stage (fig. 81).

Sukeroku is searching for a lost sword named Tomokirimaru. For this reason, he has been picking quarrels indiscriminately in the Yoshiwara and seizing the sword of every passerby in the street to see if it is the one he seeks.

Sukeroku's brother, Shimbei, arrives. At first he remonstrates with Sukeroku for his aggressive behavior, but is satisfied by his explanation and even offers to help. This involves a certain amount of comedy as Sukeroku tries to teach his feeble brother how to fight, and they then pick on a number of passersby, forcing them to crawl between their legs. Sukeroku's mother then appears and remonstrates with Sukeroku, but she, too, is inclined to accept the justification he gives of his behavior.

Ikyū returns, and Sukeroku succeeds in provoking him into drawing his sword, which turns out to be Tomokirimaru. Having conferred with Agemaki, Sukeroku decides to ambush Ikyū later that night. Sukeroku leaves via the *hanamichi* while Agemaki watches him from the main stage.

The play normally finishes at this point, but a final scene is sometimes performed when Sukeroku kills Ikyū and then hides 129 from his pursuers in a vat of (real) water before escaping over the rooftops.

A product of the popular culture of Edo at its zenith, *Sukeroku* still delights contemporary audiences with a vibrant beauty that literature has failed to capture.

Tōkaidō Yotsuya Kaidan (Yotsuya Ghost Stories)

Written by Tsuruya Namboku IV, this "contemporary" (*sewamono*) play was first performed in 1825. The original has five acts, but the ones described here, particularly acts 2 and 3, are the most frequently performed. The plot has an interesting connection with *Kanadehon Chūshingura* (The Treasury of Loyal Retainers) in that Tamiya Iemon, the "hero," is represented as a former retainer, albeit an unfaithful one, of Enya Hangan.

Act 2, "The House of Tamiya Iemon"

Tamiya Iemon is living in poverty with his sick wife, Oiwa, who has recently given birth to a child. To earn a little money, Iemon has turned to making umbrellas.

Although poor, Iemon is extremely good-looking and Oume, the beautiful granddaughter of a wealthy neighbor, Itō Kihei, is in love with him and anxious to marry. To expedite matters, Kihei sends medicine to Oiwa. Ostensibly to cure her of her sickness, the medicine is actually intended to disfigure her sufficiently for Iemon to want to divorce her. The medicine produces the desired effect (fig. 9) and Iemon, appalled at the sight of Oiwa, walks out. In order to have grounds for divorce, Iemon bids Takuetsu, a masseur, to rape Oiwa. But Takuetsu is unable to bring himself to do so, and instead he forces Oiwa, who is unaware of the change in her appearance, to look at her face in a mirror.

Realizing that she has been a victim of a gruesome plot, Oiwa decides to visit her neighbor to "thank" him for the medicine. Before doing so, she attempts to make herself presentable by blackening her teeth and combing her hair, which, as she does so, comes away in bunches in her hand. Takuetsu attempts to stop her from leaving, and in the ensuing struggle Oiwa's throat is accidentally cut on a sword. She dies cursing Iemon.

Iemon returns and kills his servant, Kohei. To make it look as if Kohei and Oiwa were lovers who have committed suicide together, Iemon nails their bodies on opposite sides of a board, which he throws into a river.

This is one of the more horrific scenes in Kabuki, possessing an eery beauty that is enhanced by the smoke from a coil of incense (intended in the play, which is set in summer, to drive away mosquitoes) and the constant crying of Oiwa's baby, which in itself can set an audience's nerves on edge. The revolving stage is also effective in showing the contrast between Iemon's hovel and the luxurious mansion next door.

Act 3, "The River Bank"

Iemon marries Oume but kills her on their wedding night, the result of Oiwa's curse. To escape Oiwa's vengeful spirit, Iemon attempts to go into hiding, but while fishing one day he hooks the board with the bodies of his wife and Kohei, and these appear to come briefly to life (figs. 82, 83). Traditionally, the roles of Kohei and Oiwa are performed by the same actor.

82–83. *Tōkaidō Yotsuya Kaidan*, act 3, "The River Bank." Iemon hooks a heavy object while fishing. On closer inspection it turns out to be the board onto which he had previously nailed his wife. When Iemon looks again at the body, it has become a skeleton.

Act 5, "Snake Mountain"

Iemon is tormented nightly by the ghost of Oiwa, which also causes the deaths of his parents. Iemon himself is eventually killed by Yomoshichi to avenge Iemon's many murders, including Yomoshichi's own wife, the sister of Oiwa.

Ukare Bōzu (The Mischievous Priest)

Under a different title, this dance was first performed as one of a group of seven in 1811. It was revived with the present title in 1929. The musical accompaniment is in the narrative (*kiyomoto*) style.

Ukare Bōzu portrays a type of beggar-priest common in the Edo period. On receipt of a small amount of money, he would perform religious austerities for other people, particularly that of pouring cold water over one's self. Consequently, the dancer is naked except for a loincloth and a thin transparent coat of gauze and carries a wooden bucket (fig. 84). The dance itself is amusing and full of variety.

One section of particular interest is that called *mazekoze* ("potpourri"), in which the performer imitates, in quick succession, a boatman, the murder of Yoichibei by Sadakurō (from act 5 of *Kanadehon Chūshingura*), a girl playing battledore and shuttlecock, a strolling female singer, a sailing ship, and a street vendor selling butterflies.

84. *Ukare Bōzu*. The beggar priest dances with a bucket and staff.

Yoshitsune Sembon Zakura (Yoshitsune and the Thousand Cherry Trees)

This five-act "historical" (_jidaimono_) play, adapted from the Bunraku theater, was first staged in 1747. The playwrights were Takeda Izumo II, Miyoshi Shōraku, and Namiki Senryū.

Japan in the twelfth century was divided by the civil wars between the rival Genji and Heike clans. After a period of ascendancy, the Heike were annihilated by the Genji in a series of encounters that culminated in the great sea battle of Dan-no-Ura in 1185. Instrumental in the defeat of the Heike was the young Genji general Yoshitsune. Brilliant as Yoshitsune's military exploits were, however, they only incurred the jealous wrath of the his elder half-brother, Yoritomo, the leader of the Genji clan. Yoshitsune was forced to flee for his life, and this flight, and the legendary adventures it involved, has been the subject of many plays and dances in the repertoire of traditional Japanese theater, including _Yoshitsune Sembon Zakura_, one of the greatest Kabuki dramas deriving from the Bunraku theater. Despite the title, Yoshitsune is not the hero of the play, although he does appear in a secondary capacity in those parts of the play with which he is directly connected. Other important characters in this part of the play are Yoshitsune's lover, the dancer Shizuka, and the fox which, possessing supernatural powers, disguises itself as Yoshitsune's loyal retainer, Satō Tadanobu.

The remainder of the play consists of a number of plots related to the Heike generals Taira no Tomomori, Taira no Koremori, and Taira no Noritsune, actual historical personages who died at Dan-no-Ura but who have been made to survive for the purposes of the play. They first appear disguised as commoners waiting for the day when they will rise up and avenge themselves on the Genji.

Act 1, "The Mansion of Yoshitsune at Horikawa, Kyoto"

After his victory at the battle of Ichinotani, Yoshitsune sent three heads to Yoritomo claiming falsely that they were those of the Heike generals Tomomori, Koremori, and Noritsune. Yoshitsune has also accepted the gift of a drum from the emperor 133

85. *Yoshitsune Sembon Zakura*, act 2, scene 1, "The Inari Fox Shrine at Fushimi." Both with an arm extended, Tadanobu (left) and Benkei separate the two lovers, Shizuka and Yoshitsune.

and married the daughter of a Heike leader.

Suspicious of Yoshitsune's motives, Yoritomo sends an emissary to question him. Yoshitsune answers the questions satisfactorily, but a troop of soldiers, also sent by Yoritomo, arrives and attacks the mansion. Anxious not to antagonize his brother, Yoshitsune does not retaliate, but Benkei kills the attackers singlehanded, including the leaders, collects their heads in a barrel of rainwater, and stirs them around as if he were washing potatoes.

Act 2, scene 1, "The Inari Fox Shrine at Fushimi"

Because of Benkei's impetuosity, reconciliation with Yoritomo is now impossible. Yoshitsune has fled the capital and is now preparing to leave by ship for Kyushu in the south. Yoshitsune admonishes Benkei and refuses permission to his own lover, Lady Shizuka, to accompany them on their journey. To console and protect her, Yoshitsune gives her the precious drum named Hatsune, presented to him by the emperor.

Left alone, Shizuka is captured by the comic Hayami no Tōta and his men, who are in pursuit of Yoshitsune. Shizuka is rescued, however, by Satō Tadanobu, one of Yoshitsune's loyalest retainers.

Yoshitsune returns, praises Tadanobu and, presenting him with a suit of his own armor, orders him to look after and pro-

134   tect Shizuka (fig. 85). The role of Tadanobu is performed in the

"rough" *aragoto* style. The famous exit he performs reveals that he is not the real Tadanobu but a fox in disguise, anxious to lay hands on the drum, the skin of which has been fashioned from the hides of its parents.

Act 2, scene 2, "The House of the Boatman, Tokaiya Gimpei"
Yoshitsune and his party go to nearby Daimotsu, where they hire a ship from Gimpei to ferry them across to Kyushu. Bad weather delays them, however, and it turns out that Gimpei is the Heike general Taira no Tomomori in disguise, who is waiting for a chance to take his revenge on Yoshitsune for the defeat of his clan. Gimpei's wife, Oryū, is actually the court lady Suke no Tsubone, and their little "daughter," the child-emperor Antoku. When Yoshitsune and the others have left for the ship, Gimpei is revealed as Tomomori, dressed in white and silver armor. Announcing that he will attack Yoshitsune when they have put to sea, he leaves with an escort of sailors.

Act 2, scene 3, "The Beach at Daimotsu-ura"
Dressed in court robes, Suke no Tsubone is seen with the little emperor as well as other ladies-in-waiting as they wait for the outcome of the sea battle that is now taking place between Yoshitsune and Tomomori.

News is brought that all is not well, and when they look out to sea, they see the lights go out on Tomomori's ship, the signal of defeat. A second messenger arrives to describe the debacle and, as previously arranged, the women prepare to kill themselves.

Holding Antoku in her arms, Suke no Tsubone is herself about to jump into the sea when she is stopped by the arrival of Yoshitsune's men. Brandishing a halberd, the wounded Tomomori enters in search of the little emperor. At first intent on killing Yoshitsune, Tomomori is eventually reconciled to his enemy and entrusts Antoku to his care. Tomomori then commits suicide in spectacular fashion by tying himself to a great anchor and leaping into the sea (fig. 86).

Act 3, scene 1, "The Village of Shimo-Ichimura"
The Heike general Taira no Koremori has gone into hiding. His 135

86. *Yoshitsune Sembon Zakura*, act 2, scene 3, "The Beach at Dai-motsu-ura." Tomomori pre-pares to throw the anchor into the sea.

87. *Yoshitsune Sembon Zakura*, act 3, scene 2, "The Sushi Shop." Yazaemon (left) has stabbed Gonta. As he is dying, Gonta reveals that he is not the villain everyone thought.

wife, Wakaba no Naishi, is seen journeying in search of her husband accompanied by their small son, Rokudai, and a retainer, Kokingo. Stopping to rest beneath a pasania tree, they fall foul of the villainous Igami no Gonta who, after ingratiating himself with the child by collecting pasania nuts for him, then extorts money from them. Genji forces come searching for them, but Kokingo manages to fight them off until he is finally mortally wounded. Before dying, Kokingo tells Wakaba to go the house of Yazaemon, a Heike supporter, in a nearby village. Later, Yazaemon himself passes by and, noticing Kokingo's body, cuts off the head, intending to pass it off as that of Koremori, whom he wishes to protect.

Act 3, scene 2, "The Sushi Shop"

Yazaemon turns out to be the owner of a sushi shop and the father of the reprobate Gonta. The Heike general Taira no Koremori is hiding there disguised as the young apprentice Yasuke. Unaware of Yasuke's real identity, Yazaemon's daughter, Osato, has fallen in love with him and is anxious to marry.

Gonta arrives, wheedles money out of his aged mother, and is about to leave when he notices his father, Yazaemon, returning. Not wishing to be seen, Gonta hides the money in one of three sushi buckets, situated side by side on the stage, and withdraws. Yazaemon then enters and hides the head he is carrying in the bucket adjacent to the one containing the money. The confusion over the contents of the buckets is the clue to what follows.

That night, Wakaba no Naishi and Rokudai (Koremori's wife and child) arrive. Realizing who Yasuke is, Gonta rushes off to inform the Genji authorities and claim a reward. Intending to take the bucket containing his money, he mistakenly takes that with the head.

Yazaemon starts to make after Gonta to stop him, but only runs into the Genji general Kajiwara, who demands the head of Koremori. Unaware of its actual contents, Yazaemon is about to open the bucket containing the money when Gonta arrives with the head together with two people who appear to be Wakaba 137 and Rokudai, bound and gagged. Kajiwara accepts the head as that of Koremori and leaves with his prisoners (Wakaba and Rokudai).

Appalled at Gonta's treachery, Yazaemon stabs him. In a Kabuki convention called *modori* ("return"), according to which a seemingly bad character turns out to be good, Gonta reveals that the prisoners earlier led away were his own wife and child, whom he had sacrificed to save the real Wakaba and Rokudai (fig. 87). In addition, the head had been Kokingo's, not that of Koremori, who then enters, safe and sound, with his wife and child. Gonta dies vindicated in what is regarded as one of the great loyalty scenes of Kabuki.

Act 4, scene 1, "The Journey to Mt. Yoshino"

In what is often performed as an independent dance, Yoshitsune's lover Lady Shizuka and his loyal retainer Satō Tadanobu (the fox in disguise) make their way to be reunited with Yoshitsune in his place of hiding on Mt. Yoshino. Stopping on the way, and with the cherry trees in full bloom, the fox-Tadanobu comforts Shizuka by teaching her a folk dance. The high point

88. *Yoshitsune Sembon Zakura*, act 4, scene 2, "The Mansion of Kawatsura Hōgen on Mt. Yoshino." Tadanobu poses in a backbend as Shizuka threatens him with a sword.

of this episode is Tadanobu's own dance in which he recalls the death of the elder brother of the real Tadanobu at the battle of Yashima.

Act 4, scene 2, "The Mansion of Kawatsura Hōgen on Mt. Yoshino"

There is much confusion when the real Tadanobu arrives, only to be followed by the fox-Tadanobu and Shizuka. To ascertain who is the real Tadanobu, Shizuka strikes the drum and the fox appears through the staircase in the middle of the set (fig. 88). In a scene which involves the actor in the role wearing a special fox costume, speaking in a "fox" voice, and making animal gestures, the fox reveals its true identity and explains how it is anxious to be given the drum since it is made from the hide of its parents. As a reward for having guarded Shizuka so well, Yoshitsune gives the drum to the delighted fox. At that moment, Heike forces under Taira no Noritsune attack the mansion disguised as warrior-priests. But the fox, out of gratitude to Yoshitsune, bewitches them and drives them away.

Yowa Nasake Ukina no Yokogushi (Scarred Yosaburō)

A "contemporary" (*sewamono*) masterpiece of the late Edo period, this play was written by Segawa Jokō III and first staged in 1853. The original work is a long one consisting of nine acts and eighteen scenes altogether, but nowadays only acts 2 and 4 are regularly performed.

Act 2, "The Beach at Kisarazu"

Yosaburō, the adopted son of the proprietor of the Izuya in Nihombashi, goes to Kisarazu to recover his health. Walking on the beach one day, he encounters Otomi, the mistress of a gangster boss in the area, and falls in love with her at first sight. Oblivious to everything except the beautiful girl, Yosaburō's jacket falls to the sand. The scene ends with a typical "contemporary" (*sewamono*) touch as Yosaburō stares after the girl, not realizing that he has picked up his jacket and put it on back to front.

139

89. *Yowa Nasake Ukina no Yokogushi*, act 4, "Genjidana." Otomi reacts in disbelief as Yosaburō reveals who he is.

In the following scene, not normally performed, Yosaburō meets secretly with Otomi, but they are discovered by the girl's irate lover, who wounds Yosaburō by cutting his face and body and then throws him, half dead, into the sea.

Act 4, "Genjidana"

Yosaburō has survived the attack on him, but his body is scarred in thirty-four different places. During the three years that have passed since the incident took place, he has become a petty criminal specializing in extortion. Together with his accomplice, Kōmori Yasu, Yosaburō comes to Otomi's house to extort money from her, not realizing who she is. Amazed at finding Otomi alive and well, Yosaburō reveals, in a famous speech, who he is and bitterly laments the chance encounter with her that brought about his downfall (fig. 89).

Set in the downtown district of Edo, this act is replete with the decadent atmosphere of the later Edo period. It is usually performed according to an acting tradition believed to have been established by Nakamura Nakazō, in which Yosaburō's accomplice, Kōmori Yasu, wears a woman's kimono and has a tattoo of a bat on his cheek. Another feature is the cloth that Yosaburō wears stylishly about his head to hide his scars. For, despite his having become a petty thief, Yosaburō still has about him the qualities of the son of a wealthy merchant.

WHERE TO SEE KABUKI AND HOW TO OBTAIN TICKETS

[Kabuki performances are often daylong affairs, with the morning and evening shows of different content and requiring separate tickets. This matter, as well as the time when performances begin and end, should be inquired into when tickets are purchased.]

TOKYO

Kabuki-za

Ginza 4-12-15, Chūō-ku, Tokyo. Tel. 03-541-3131. Walk from Higashi Ginza Station on the Hibiya Line. Tickets are available at the theater's ticket window or "playguide" ticket agencies throughout the city. Reservations can be made by telephoning the theater up to and including the day of performance.

National Theater

Hayabusa-chō 4-1, Chiyoda-ku, Tokyo. Tel. 03-265-7411. Walk from Nagatachō Station on the Yurakuchō Line. Tickets are available at the theater's ticket window or "playguide" ticket agencies throughout the city. Reservations can be made by telephoning the theater up to three days before the performance.

Shimbashi Embu-jō

Ginza 6-18-2, Chūō-ku, Tokyo. Tel 03-541-2211. Walk from Higashi Ginza Station on the Hibiya Line. Tickets are available from the theater's ticket window or "playguide" ticket agencies throughout the cities. Reservations can be made by telephoning the theater up to and including the day of the performance. 141

KYOTO

Minami-za

Shijō Ōhashi Higashi-zume, Higashiyama-ku, Kyoto. Tel. 075-561-1155. Walk from Shijō Station on the Keihan Line. Tickets are available from the theater's ticket window or "playguide" ticket agencies throughout the city. Reservations can be made by telephoning the theater up to and including the day before the performance.

OSAKA

Naka-za

Dōtombori 1-7-19, Minami-ku, Osaka. Tel. 06-211-1566. Walk from Namba Station on the Kintetsu Line. Tickets are available from the theater's ticket window or "playguide" ticket agencies throughout the city. Reservations can be made by telephoning the theater up to and including the day before the performance.

Shin Kabuki-za

Namba 4-3-25, Minami-ku, Osaka. Tel. 06-631-2121. Walk from Namba Station on the Midōsuji Line. Tickets are available from the theater's ticket window or "playguide" ticket agencies throughout the city. Reservations can be made by telephoning the theater up to one week before the performance.

NAGOYA

Misono-za

Sakae 1-16-14, Naka-ku, Nagoya. Tel. 052-211-1451. Walk from Fushimi Station on the Higashiyama Line. Tickets are available from the theater's ticket window or "playguide" ticket agencies throughout the city. Reservations can be made by telephoning the theater up to and including the day of the performance. October is the only month in which Kabuki is performed at this theater.

ENGLISH/JAPANESE LIST
OF PLAY TITLES

[This alphabetical listing is based on the English titles of the plays discussed in the section "Thirty-six Plays: Synopses and Highlights," in which the plays are arranged in alphabetical order by their Japanese titles. Numbers indicate the page on which a particular synopsis begins. For an alphabetized listing based on the Japanese titles, see the table of contents.]